ORIGINAL OHIO

ORIGINAL OHIO

Dreamsville, the Magic City & Other Historic Ohio Communities

David Meyers and Elise Meyers Walker

Published by The History Press
Charleston, SC
www.historypress.com

Cover images: Top row: German Village. *Authors' photo*; Ripley. *Authors' photo*; and Mariemont. *Ford Walker photo*. The black-and-white photo courtesy of Jaite, Library of Congress. Back cover: Roscoe Village. *Authors' photo*.

First published 2024

Manufactured in the United States

ISBN 9781467156233

Library of Congress Control Number: 2023949157

Notice: The information in this book is true and complete to the best of our knowledge. It is offered without guarantee on the part of the authors or The History Press. The authors and The History Press disclaim all liability in connection with the use of this book.

CONTENTS

ACKNOWLEDGEMENTS

Thanks to the following people for their assistance and support: Beverly Meyers, Sam Walker, Nyla Vollmer, Dewey Johnson, Randy McNutt, Gretchen Colon, John Rodrigue and Katie Parry. This book is dedicated to the memory of Joseph P. "Joe" Sears, my friend since second grade.

Introduction

THE DREAMERS AND THE DREAMS

Every community begins with a dream—and a dreamer. It has been that way since the first colonists came to the New World from the Old. And there is no reason to believe that it was any different for those who preceded them and carved their ancient signatures on the land. All of them, undoubtedly, dreamed for a better life.

Ohio wasn't exactly a blank canvas when the first Europeans arrived. It was bestrewn with more than ten thousand earthworks of various sizes and descriptions—some burial, others ceremonial—left behind by an unknown people who came to be called the mound builders. These mysterious cultures were contemporaries of the pharaohs who built the pyramids of Egypt.[1] But by 1650—twenty years before the French explorer La Salle "discovered" the Ohio River—they had all vanished.[2] Or had they?

The earliest missionaries to the Ohio Territory identified six major groups of "Indians"—the Shawnees, Seneca-Cayugas, Delawares (Leni Lenapes), Wyandots, Ottawas and Myaamia (Miamis).[3] They began arriving in the area during the 1700s, some having originally been driven out by the Iroquois. The Shawnees, in fact, may have been descended from a mound building culture, although one of their leaders, Hokolesqua (aka "Cornstalk"), purportedly said that the earthworks had been built by an ancient race of white people. Maybe that's just what he thought the white men wanted to hear.

For many years, the European settlers preferred to believe that the mound builders were a lost race who had no connection to the "primitive savages" who now occupied the land. This helped bolster the belief that displacing them was in keeping with Manifest Destiny—the idea that it was God's plan for the United States to expand throughout the North American continent, spreading the tripartite gospels of Christianity, democracy and capitalism. The fact that the American Indians sided with the British during the Revolutionary War just made matters worse for them.

Philosopher John Locke believed that the "wild Indian" in America did not share the European's understanding of property rights. He was wrong. As Livia Gershon has noted, "The idea of pre-Columbian America as a universal commons is a myth."[4] Among "the Iroquois and Algonquian nations," for example, "women in a particular family typically owned specific maize fields."[5] Sometimes they even allocated designated hunting grounds to specific families. And they signed treaties with the government of the United States with the expectation that their property rights would be protected.

Even though there had already been some European settlement in Ohio, the Northwest Ordinance of 1787 provided for the survey and sale of lands north and west of the Ohio River. Eight years later, the Treaty of Greenville established the boundaries of Indian Territory, encouraging new settlement on parcels of land ceded by the Native Americans as they were pushed farther west.

At the time Ohio became a state in 1803, there were numerous Native American villages dotting the landscape. But despite or, sometimes, because of various Indian treaties, the tribes were soon expelled from the state. However, as Dr. Barbara Mann has pointed out, "A tremendous number of Indigenous people remained in Ohio after Removal."[6] When they refused to migrate to the lands designated for them in the West, "the government simply declared those people no longer Indian."[7]

Bill Moose was thought to be the last full-blooded member of the Wyandot tribe to live in Ohio.[8] In 1843, when he was five years old, his family refused to leave when the federal government removed the Wyandots to Kansas. Instead, they relocated from Upper Sandusky to a spot just north of Columbus. Bill spent much of his life in a shack on the edge of the neighborhood of Clintonville. Upon his passing in 1937, a few months shy of his 100th birthday, an estimated twenty thousand people attended his memorial service.

Following the War of 1812, many New Englanders began abandoning the long-settled towns and villages on the Eastern Seaboard in order to take advantage of cheap land in the West. They came in droves, leaving the comforts of the civilized world to seek their fortune in the wilderness. It was called "Ohio Fever," and as historian Harlan Hatcher noted, "It was one of the largest and most homogeneous mass migrations in American history"—with an emphasis on homogenous.[9]

As a result, the population of Ohio increased dramatically from 45,365 people in 1800 to 230,760 in 1810, or 408 percent. Between 1810 and 1820, it increased another 152 percent, reaching 581,295. By 1860, just before the start of the Civil War, the state had just over 2.3 million residents. Today, it is approaching 12 million, many of whom live in its 250 cities and 688 villages. And many of these communities started as someone's dream.

This book is a chronological account of selected towns and villages that illustrates how the state was settled over the course of six centuries. The ones we have chosen to highlight were, arguably, all planned to some extent, whether formally (e.g., Mariemont) or through the convergence of like-minded individuals (e.g., Ripley). But more importantly, there is still something to see of the original architecture (or, in a two instances, a credible replica).

As we discussed in a previous book, *Historic Black Settlements of Ohio*, many free or formerly enslaved women and children also made their home in Ohio, establishing more than one hundred colonies or hamlets prior to the Civil War. Yet there is little physical evidence of them. And while dozens of pioneering log cabins have been preserved throughout the state, nothing remains of, say, the famous longhouses of the Shawnees or other structures from Native American villages that sometimes contained several hundred dwellings.

So, the two earliest communities we discuss, both of which were occupied by Native Americans, were rebuilt or are being rebuilt from the ground up. Others have been preserved or even restored to some degree. And a few—perhaps more than a few—are disappearing and will be lost unless some action is taken in the near future. But at present, they all provide an opportunity to take a stroll or drive through history.

We sometimes forget that history is all around us, often because we have no idea what that history is. Some places are considered historic because of what occurred. Other are considered historic because they are simply old. We like both, but we could not write about them all. Instead, we have selected a few of our favorites in the hope that others will love them as much as we do—and maybe spend some time and dollars visiting them so they won't be as apt to fade away.

—DAVID MEYERS

Chapter 1

SUNWATCH INDIAN VILLAGE, CIRCA 1250

Dayton, Montgomery County

"The Ash Heap of History"

Located just south of Dayton on the western floodplain of the Great Miami River in Montgomery County, SunWatch—as archaeologists named it—is the best-known Fort Ancient Indian village in the United States. The fact that it was previously called the Incinerator Site suggests just how close it came to being totally erased from history. Instead, the settlement is in the process of being gradually reconstructed as more information is unearthed—literally—from the ash heap of history.

The three mound building traditions in Ohio—Adena, Hopewell and Fort Ancient—were named by those who came afterward. However, little is known about them or their relationship to one another. Believed to be descended from the Hopewell culture, the Fort Ancient people were the last of the mound builders. The Adena culture was the earliest.

The Fort Ancient people lived in southern Ohio during the years 1000–1750 in villages that numbered from one hundred to five hundred inhabitants.[10] So, in truth, the Europeans just missed them and likely encountered some without knowing it. Judging by the skeletons that have been disinterred, the Fort Ancient men averaged five feet, three inches tall and the women five feet, one inch.

Located at the convergence of the prairie, river and woodlands, SunWatch was an agrarian community, raising corn, squash, gourds, sunflowers, beans and tobacco (the last for ceremonial purposes). They also fished and hunted

A reconstructed SunWatch Village is slowly taking shape. *Andrew Sawyer/Wikipedia.*

turkey, deer, elk and black bear. It is believed that SunWatch was occupied for at least fifteen and possibly as many as forty years before being abandoned. The site was never reoccupied.

As early as the 1930s, however, local farmers began turning up numerous prehistoric artifacts with their plows. Soon these items came to the attention of Indian relic collectors, who began scouring the fields for other evidence of Indigenous peoples.

The acreage was previously owned by the Vance family (1853–1941), and a grandson eventually sold it to the City of Dayton. During the period 1964–70, amateur archaeologists John Allman and Charles Smith "conducted fairly extensive excavations uncovering more than 14 burials, numerous storage pits, hearths and post holes as well as thousands of pieces of pottery and stone, bone, antler and shell tools."[11] But there was much more to be discovered.

When plans were announced in the early 1970s to expand the nearby sewage treatment plant, Allman and Smith took their concerns to James Heilman, curator of anthropology at the Dayton Museum of Natural History. Salvage excavations were immediately undertaken in an effort to recover as much information as possible before the site was lost. Fortunately, as the importance of dig became apparent, Dayton officials decided to set aside the land for further research.

SunWatch was nothing if not a planned community. Archaeologists were able to determine that it was a circular, three-acre village surrounded by a palisade and may have held as many as 250 people. Author David Hurst Thomas observed, "The main plaza, an oval area about 190 feet across was kept clean of trash and pits. A wolf burial was found here, accompanied by some wolf tooth ornaments; an effigy wolf-man pipe [one side of the bowl was the face of a wolf, the other the face of a man] was found, suggesting to some that the wolf was a clan symbol or legendary ancestor to the SunWatch people."[12]

The village included an open central plaza with a "stockade of irregularly spaced wooden poles [surrounding] the core of the village."[13] The overall shape of the village was slightly oval. A tall pole stood in the middle with approximately twenty-five to thirty houses grouped around it. They averaged sixteen by twenty feet square. Some of them were reconstructed using the wattle-and-daub technique as a technological experiment. But as archaeologist Chris Turnbow discovered when he lived in one of them for a week, the thatched roof was a very poor insulator against Ohio winters. He suggested that they may have moved elsewhere in the in the winter or occupied wigwams.

"Because the inside of these houses were dark and smoky," Thomas wrote,

> *many household chores were done outside, in front of the houses. A wooden mortar was used to grind corn into flour. Woman also made pottery, dressed skins, sewed, wove baskets and textiles, and made bone tools. Fortunately for the archaeologists, the tools and byproducts of these activities were often dropped on the ground or swept into nearby trash pits.*[14]

The center pole—known as a gnomon—was a red cedar trunk about two feet in diameter and possibly forty feet high or more. "Because the sun occupies different positions in the sky at different points in the day and also at different times of the year, the shadow that this large central pole casts will change."[15] Much like a sundial, the shadow would sweep around the village, aligning with important village structures, creating "an astronomical calendar complex."[16] This was the same principle discovered at Woodhenge, located at Cahokia Mounds in Illinois.

Just northwest of the center post were four shorter posts arranged perpendicularly to it. There is speculation that this arrangement might have served as a solar calendar and that particular events were scheduled according to their alignment with particular stars.

Along the western edge was a building the archaeologists nicknamed the "Big House." They suspect it was either where the chief lived or, more likely, a communal structure that may have been the focus of the religious and political life at SunWatch. "Judging from similar structures recorded by early explorers and missionaries," Thomas noted, "this council house was probably decorated with posts carved with human faces, turtles, and snakes. On the walls were brightly painted murals. Masks, pipes, sacred bundles, and costumes were stored in the rear room."[17]

On April 29 and again on August 14, the shadow from the center pole enters the doorway of the Big House and lines up with the fire hearth. In fact, the hearth is not positioned in the center of the house but rather is offset to the south. Archaeologists suspect that April 29 would have been when the Fort Ancient people planted maize using hoes made of mussel shells, and August 14—110 days later—would have been when they harvested it.

The inhabitants of SunWatch are believed to have cultivated as many as 150 acres. Maize was such an important staple of their diet that it has been estimated it provided 75 percent of their caloric intake. Adjacent to the Big House was another structure nicknamed the "Solstice House." On December 21—the morning of the winter solstice—the shadow cast by the gnomon would align with the center of the Solstice House doorway.

Several other wood and thatch huts have been re-created, including dwellings, all on their original sites. They also cultivated gardens and native prairie. Systematic excavation has revealed through "excellent bone and charred macrobotanical preservation" an unparalleled picture of life in a Native American village circa 1250.[18] This has led to partial restoration of the village, which is operated by the Dayton Society of Natural History as an open-air museum and interpretive center. The goal is to eventually rebuild the entire village.

In 1990, SunWatch was designated a National Historic Landmark. While there are many archaeological sites open to visitors throughout the country, they are very few that are being reconstructed in place. It also represents an almost unheard-of collaboration between archaeologists and representatives of Indigenous peoples to ensure that any skeletal artifacts that turn up are treated with due respect.

Rather than having to use your imagination to visualize what SunWatch might have looked like in the thirteenth century, you are free to walk through history. The interpretative center provides the public with information regarding the structures and gardens, as well as the restoration of the native prairie. There is even a reconstructed dog burial. And the museum also houses an impressive collection of artifacts that were recovered at the site. All in all, SunWatch is the perfect place to begin a tour of Ohio's historic communities.

Chapter 2

SCHOENBRUNN VILLAGE, 1772

Schoenbrunn, Tuscarawas County

"Beautiful Spring"

Schoenbrunn in Tuscarawas County is said to be the first "white" settlement in Ohio, but that is an oversimplification. It was founded in 1772 by David Zeisberger, a Moravian missionary who had been working among the Indigenous peoples in partnership with John Heckewelder.[19] As a result, the settlement contained few white (i.e., European) people, but apparently some with mixed European/Native American ancestry.

Zeisberger came to the Ohio Country from Pennsylvania with the intent of establishing a new home for "his Pennsylvania Indian converts and to further carry on his missionary work in this virgin territory."[20] He was accompanied by five families—twenty-eight people in all. When he was examining the site for its suitability, Zeisberger saw embankments along the Muskingum River that he believed were the walls of an ancient earthwork. "None of the mounds found in this county were peculiarly striking in form or size," an early historian wrote, "nor are these relics so numerous as in some other counties in Southeastern Ohio."[21] Although the first settlers were careful to preserve the mounds, later arrivals were much more cavalier in their attitudes, and many were destroyed.

The Moravian church dates back to 1457. It was founded by John Hus, who disagreed with some practices of the Roman Catholic Church and started what was originally called the Hussite movement, anticipating Martin Luther by about fifty years. As the Moravian Church, it embarked on an

Schoenbrunn Village is one of the most serene spots in Ohio. *Authors' photo.*

international missionary movement that brought Zeisberger from Moravia (i.e., Czech Republic) and Heckewelder from England to the American colonies. They immediately set about converting the native peoples.

Once they became Moravian Christians, the Indians renounced violence in any form. Consequently, they were subjected to persecution by various groups that distrusted them simply because they refused to take sides. Invited by Chief Netawatwes of the Delaware tribe to locate on the Tuscarawas River, Zeisberger and his followers set about building the settlement of Schoenbrunn—German for "beautiful spring." It "contained 60 cabins in addition to numerous huts and tepees, as well as a school, a church and a cemetery."[22] These were the first school and church erected west of the Allegheny Mountains. Not only did the school serve both boys and girls, but the Moravians also translated the Bible into the Delaware (or Lenape) language.

The Moravian Indians also established the first civil code in what would become the state of Ohio. One of the laws stated, "We will not admit rum or any other intoxicating liquor in our towns. If strangers or traders bring intoxicating liquor, the helpers shall take it from them and not restore it until the owners are ready to leave the place."[23]

Before the year was out, Zeisberger had founded a second village in the Tuscarawas Valley, Gnadenhütten. Located just ten miles south of

Schoenbrunn, Gnadenhütten meant "huts of grace" in German. It was originally led by Joshua, a Mohican chief who had become a Christian. Here on July 4, 1773, John Lewis Roth became the first white child known to have been born in the Ohio Country. Other mission settlements followed—Lichtenau, Salem and Goshen. Like the Indigenous people at SunWatch, those at Schoenbrunn hunted, fished and planted corn, beans and squash, as well as potatoes and turnips.

Over the next five years, Zeisberger continued his missionary work in the region and enjoyed much success in making Christians of the Indigenous peoples. However, with the onset of the American Revolution, the residents of Schoenbrunn found themselves "in the untenable position of a buffer territory between the British at Detroit and the Americans at Pittsburgh."[24]

When the Shawnees sided with the British early in 1777, the "non-Christians Munsees were determined to destroy the missions and murder the missionaries and Christian Indians."[25] The Munsees were a subtribe of the Lenapes or Delawares, who had a reputation for being the most warlike. Their principal totem was the wolf. They had originally driven Zeisberger's converts out of Pennsylvania.

On April 19, 1777, Zeisberger and his flock met in the church. After reaffirming their commitment to nonviolence, they all knelt while "Zeisberger offered a prayer committing the company to the protection of God and interceding with Heaven for their enemies, the Munsees."[26] They then tore down their church so it wouldn't be desecrated and totally abandoned Schoenbrunn.

"By 1777, when the British and other Native Americans forced abandonment of the settlement, it had about 400 inhabitants; sixty log structures had been built, including a Gemeinhaus [community house] and a school."[27] Before the year was out, "hostile Indians incited by the British burned the entire village, and brought to a tragic end the most dramatic mission to the Indians before the close of the eighteenth century."[28]

During 1778, Zeisberger consolidated his missions at Lichtenau, but in April 1779, he reestablished the village of Gnadenhütten, hoping to ride out the war unmolested, but to no avail. Soon the British authorities forced them to relocate north to the Sandusky River. According to historian Helen Hunt Jackson, they were "suspicious that the influence of the Moravian missionaries was thrown on the side of the colonies, and that their villages were safe centres of information and supplies."[29]

Commanded by English officers, the "savages"—non-Christian Indians who were hostile toward the Moravians—"drove them forward like cattle…

the white brethren and sisters in the midst, surrounded by the believing Indians."[30] Over the course of a month, they compelled the group through the wilds until they reached Sandusky Creek, where they were abandoned without any provisions except utensils for making maple syrup. Without bedding or blankets, they quickly built huts of logs and bark to protect them from the elements.

"In November, Governor [Arent] De Peyster, the English commander at Fort Detroit, summoned the missionaries to appear before him and refute the accusations brought against their congregations of having aided and abetted the colonies."[31] Although he had presumed them to be guilty, he became convinced of their innocence and publicly declared that they could return to their congregations. He provided them not only with passports back to Sandusky but also with his permission for them to continue their work of Christianizing the Indigenous people without interference.

"The forced evacuation of the Moravians from Schoenbrunn in 1777 led to the abandonment of Gnadenhütten in 1781," historian James Kornwolf wrote.[32] Faced with serious food shortages, Zeisberger sent a group of his followers back to Gnadenhütten, a journey of 125 miles. He charged them with the task of harvesting whatever of frozen corn crops they could. Although they remained apprehensive and planned to hide in the woods, while they were en route "they were met by some of their brethren from Schonbrun [*sic*], who advised them to go back openly into their deserted towns, assuring them that the Americans were friendly to them now," according to Jackson.[33] So they did.

However, on March 8, 1782, the very day they had planned to start their return trip, a group of one hundred to two hundred U.S. militia from Pennsylvania, led by David Williamson, slaughtered ninety-six of their number—primarily from the Lenape and Mohican tribes. After first telling the Moravian Indians that they were going to relocate them so they would not be in harm's way, Williamson's men then informed them they would be executed as spies.

Although the Native Americans vehemently denied the charges, they asked only that they be permitted to pray and worship the night before the sentence was to be carried out. Eighteen of the militiamen refused to participate in the atrocities and removed themselves from the scene.

The following morning, Williamson's militia carried out the executions:

> *One of the party, now taking up a cooper's mallet which lay in the house, saying, "How exactly this will answer for the purpose," began*

> *with Abraham, and continued knocking down one after another until he counted fourteen that he had killed with his own hands. He now handed the instrument to one of his fellow-murderers, saying: "My arm fails me. Go on in the same way. I think I have done pretty well."*[34]

Similar scenes occurred throughout the village as the Moravian Indians continued to sing hymns and encourage and console one another as they were slain. Although they continued to plead for their lives, none of them resisted their executioners. Forty of the victims were adult men, twenty were women and thirty-four were children. Only two boys, both about fourteen, escaped, one of them having revived after he was scalped. Afterward, the entire village was burned to the ground by militia.

Zeisberger declared the Moravian Indians at Gnadenhütten all martyrs to Christianity. However, an account of the massacre in the *Pennsylvania Gazette* of April 17, 1782, claimed that the Indians had "collected a large quantity of provisions to supply their war-parties."[35] They were purportedly surprised by one hundred men who swam the river at night, then killed and scalped ninety of them, forty of whom were warriors. They then captured eighty horses, loaded them with plunder—mostly furs and skins—and returned home without losing a man.

Williamson and his men are thought to have committed the outrage in retaliation for the murder of some white settlers by another tribe a few weeks earlier. Afterward, he planned to slay the residents of Schoenbrunn as well, but one resident of that village had arrived at Gnadenhütten shortly after the soldiers had killed Joseph Schebosch, a Moravian of mixed Welsh and Lenape ancestry, and rushed back to Schoenbrunn to warn Zeisberger.

Although the massacre at Gnadenhütten is sometimes rationalized as a mistake, Williamson and his men then went on to butcher some forty peaceful Delaware Indians who were living at Killbuck Island near Fort Pitt. His actions would later result in Colonel William Crawford being burned at the stake in retaliation for the Gnadenhütten massacre.

"Outraged by the 1782 massacre of faithful pacifists," historian Frances Kennedy wrote, "the U.S. Congress in 1785 granted Moravians three town sites."[36] Then, in 1792, the British government gave the surviving Moravian Indians a tract of land in Ontario, Canada. Here they founded Fairfield or Moraviantown, only to have it destroyed by the Americans in 1813 during the Battle of the Thames.

Fortunately, in 1798, David Zeisberger led Ontario Moravians back to Ohio, where he founded the Goshen mission near the former site of

Schoenbrunn. He died there ten years later. More than a century afterward, Theodore Roosevelt pronounced the massacre "a stain on frontier character that the lapse of time cannot wash away."[37]

When European settlers began arriving in what became Tuscarawas County, they were quick to occupy the abandoned mission sites because the land was already cleared. For 146 years, crops were planted and harvested on the former site of Schoenbrunn without anyone realizing its significance. But in 1923, Joseph E. Weinland, pastor of the Dover Moravian Church, set out to locate the site of the lost village. He was soon joined by Luther and O.J. Demuth, who worked side by side with him until their goal was achieved.

One rule of the Moravian church was that a yearly report be sent to the church headquarters in Bethlehem, Pennsylvania, by each missionary in the field. It was there in the Moravian Archives that Weinland found Zeisberger's diary from 1772 to 1777, as well as other records that provided a detailed history of life in Schoenbrunn during its brief existence.

More importantly, there was also a map of the village. "The plan shows two perfectly straight perpendicular streets, with the Gemeinhaus and the school, opposite, centered on the intersections; also shown are forty houses, each in the middle of its plot and set tight against the street."[38] Using the springs as a landmark, Weiland and the Demuths located a cabin site within forty-five minutes. Then, after plowing up a cornfield, they identified the fireplaces of all the remaining cabins. However, the location of the church still eluded them. But with the assistance of William C. Mills, director of the Ohio State Archaeological and Historical Society, they uncovered the church fireplace on September 4, 1923.

After that, everything else fell in place. A few days later, they disinterred a skeleton in the burial ground that proved to be that of an Indian. Eventually, forty-three graves were located and marked. However, the intrepid group had come to realize that a complete restoration of Schoenbrunn Village was beyond their means. Fortunately, the Ohio legislature responded with $10,000 to purchase the site. Other appropriations would follow.

In 1927, the Schebosch cabin was the first building to be reconstructed. Schebosch was originally a Quaker born Joseph Bull, but he joined the Moravian church, serving the Indian mission for forty-five years. The Indians gave him the name Schebosh, which meant "running water." His wife of forty-one years was a member of the Sopus tribe. Seventeen log buildings were reconstructed, including houses, a school, a church and a trading post. The cemetery, period gardens and planted fields have been restored. Today, it is serenity itself. Ten miles away, the site of the massacre at Gnadenhütten is marked by a monument, and the Moravians rebuilt the church in 1903, along with a reconstructed cooper's house.

Chapter 3

MARIETTA, 1788

Marietta, Washington County

"Putnam's Paradise"

I wish there were more New England people going to Muskingum," Colonel John May wrote to his wife in Boston on May 12, 1788.[39] Colonel May had just witnessed a profusion of boats in Pittsburgh, packed with their human cargo, floating downriver bound for Kentucky. And he was concerned that the Ohio Company's new colony would not prosper. However, many New Englanders and others would make their way to Marietta—as it would later be called—located on the banks of the Ohio River at its confluence with the Muskingum River.

Two years later, a "Gentleman" in New Orleans praised "the industry, sobriety, and good order" of the New Englanders at Marietta whom he met while traveling down the Ohio.[40] In fact, one Christian Schultz observed that Marietta was "New England in miniature."[41] Certainly, that is what General Rufus Putnam and Brigadier General Benjamin Tupper had hoped it would become. As land speculators, they had founded the Ohio Company of Associates to purchase real estate in the Northwest Territory.

In 1770, George Washington, future president of the United States, was hired to survey large tracts of land west of his home in Virginia. Just a few years later, when he was commander in chief of the Continental army, Washington shared his impressions of the Ohio Country and his ideas for settling the territory with Putnam. On March 1, 1786, Putnam, Tupper and Dr. Manasseh Cutler convened a meeting at the Bunch of Grapes Tavern

The Land Office at Campus Martius is Ohio's oldest surviving building. *Authors' photo.*

in Boston, Massachusetts, to share their vision with other parties who were interested in migrating to the West.

With Cutler as their agent, Putnam and Tupper agreed to buy 1.5 million acres of land in what would become the state of Ohio at two-thirds of a dollar per acre.[42] They were also given another 100,000 acres—the "Donation Tract"—to serve as a buffer between them and the Indigenous peoples who already lived there. Tupper had once visited the Ohio Country as a surveyor but soon returned to New England "on account of the hostility of the Indians."[43]

Then, on April 7, 1788, General Putnam and forty-seven other members of the Ohio Company of Associates landed at the site of Marietta, the first permanent settlement in the Northwest Territory. "At first the new region was known as Muskingum, and the little town as Adelphi ["Brotherhood"], but in the summer of 1788 the officers of the Ohio Company adopted the name of Marietta" in honor of Marie Antoinette, the French queen who had aided the colonies during the Revolutionary War.[44] Other names considered were Castrapolis, Protepolis, Urania, Tempe and Genesis. However, detractors called it "Putnam's Paradise" or "Cutler's Indian Heaven."[45]

On November 28, 1787, the Ohio Company sent an advance team to prepare the way for the others. Among the forty-eight men were "six boat-builders, four house-builders, one blacksmith, and nine common workmen."[46] Upon their arrival, they started laying out their new community according to the plans they had drawn up in Boston. Their families would begin to arrive within a few months.

The following June, George Washington wrote in a letter to Richard Henderson:

> *No colony in America was ever settled under such favorable auspices as that which has just commenced at the Muskingum.…If I was a young man, just preparing to begin the world, or if advanced in life and had a family to make provision for, I know of no country where I should rather fix my habitation.*[47]

The settlers quickly found evidence that another civilization had preceded theirs and now lay buried beneath the thick forest. As one historian wrote, "Rectangular and circular mounds, long lines of earthworks, proved that a race well advanced in civilization and numerous enough to co-operate in vast undertakings had once lived about the Muskingum."[48] They included a great conical mound that encompassed much of what became the initial settlement of Marietta. But the members of the Ohio Company had no idea just who these mysterious mound builders were.

One settler wrote home, "This country, for fertility of soil and pleasant of situation, not only exceeds my expectations, but exceeds any part of Europe or America that I was ever in."[49] However, there was a lot of work to be done to wrest a city out of the wilderness, beginning with the surveyors surveying the land and the guards guarding the surveyors against the threat from the so-called Indians who claimed the land as their hunting grounds. Thomas Summers would later write, "Although the Indians gave them a hearty welcome, they afterwards proved treacherous for they were not pleased to see the land cleared and the huts erected."[50]

One of the reasons for selecting this particular spot was its location just across the Muskingum River from Fort Harmar, a three-year-old military post, which offered them some protection against the Native Americans. However, Putnam decided that they should build a fort of their own, Campus Martius ("Field of Mars"). It was "a stockade or parallelogram of vertical logs set so deep in the earth" that some were dug up nearly a century later and preserved as relics.[51] Within this fortress they built cabins and offices and set about civilizing primitive Ohio.

According to one pioneer, Ichabod Nye, prior to the arrival of the Ohio Company, there was "nothing but a herd of wild Men either red or white (not much differing except in Collour) inhabiting the Countrey."[52] However, the settlers soon found a need to employ the "wild Men" to do their hunting and scouting for them, particularly as the threat of "Indian troubles" arose.[53]

The town of Marietta was laid out with reference to the Muskingum, rather than the Ohio River. The street closest to its bank was named Front Street. All the streets that ran parallel to Front Street were numbered: 2nd, 3rd, 4th and so on. Those that were at right angles to Front Street were named after Revolutionary War heroes: Greene, Butler, Putnam, Washington and so on. However, some exceptions cropped up. Initially, all the ancient earthworks were preserved by placing them in public squares.

During the summer of 1789, Joseph Buell and Levi Munsell built the first frame house in Marietta. It was intended to be a tavern. "The timber of it was prepared by Captain Enoch Shepherd at McKeesport, Pennsylvania, who made it into a raft upon which he brought his family to Marietta."[54]

The "Yankees," as the New Englanders were called, were of Puritan stock. Most of them were Congregationalists and attended services at Fort Harmar. At least fifty of them had served in the Revolutionary War. And several were clergymen, including Manasseh Cutler, who was instrumental in having $200 set aside to "for the support of preachers and schoolmasters" in the new settlements.[55] During the first winter, the children of Marietta were provided with basic schooling within the wall of Campus Martius. Then in 1798, Muskingum Academy was constructed.

In 1799, the first church was chartered in Marietta. Although it was a Congregational church, it included a number of members with different religious backgrounds. In 1807, they erected their first church building. When it burned down in 1905, they immediately constructed another one. Known as the First Congregational Church United Church of Christ, it is the longest continuously operating church west of the Allegheny Mountains.

Many of the officers and soldiers had also been members of a lodge of Freemasons, originally chartered in Massachusetts in 1775. In 1790, they revived it as the American Union Lodge of Marietta—the oldest Masonic lodge in the original Northwest Territory. However, in 1801 the house that contained the lodge room caught fire, and the charter, jewels and other regalia were apparently destroyed.

Although Marietta was settled by New Englanders, its location proved to be particularly attractive to the people who were already living on the Virginia-Pennsylvania frontier. As a result, the village of Marietta was never quite the Yankee bastion it appeared. Then, soon after its founding, southerners also began arriving, further diluting the Yankee influence.

There's quite a bit of early Ohio history still on display or underfoot in Marietta and Fort Harmar. Both historic districts are listed in the National Register of Historic Places. To begin with, there are the Marietta Earthworks. Remnants of these Hopewell or possibly Adena culture embankments and mounds can be found at various places throughout the city. Europeans gave them such Latin names as Sacra Via ("sacred way"), Quadranaou ("slab"), Capitolium ("capital") and Conus ("cone"). The last is a thirty-foot mound located in Mound Cemetery (5th and Scammel Streets). The cemetery is the final resting place of the largest number of Revolutionary War officers buried in a single location. Quadranaou and Capitolium are both in public parks.

Built in 1788, the Ohio Company Land Office (Campus Martius complex) is the oldest standing building in Ohio. Originally located on the Muskingum River, it was moved inside Campus Martius in 1791 so that it could be protected from attacks by hostile Indians who objected to the white man's invasion of their hunting grounds. It is a simple cabin with a door, two windows and a stone chimney.

The Rufus Putnam House (Campus Martius complex), once commonly called the Old Block-House, was completed in 1790. Constructed of four-inch-thick hewn oak timbers, it was later covered with clapboard. In 1795, Putnam bought an adjacent blockhouse and used the lumber to add four more rooms to the original four-room dwelling.

In 1830, Reverend Luther Bingham, a pastor at the Congregationalist Church, established the Institute for Education. However, it failed two years later. The citizens of Marietta than banded together to create the Marietta Collegiate Institute and Western Teacher's Seminary. In 1835, it was renamed Marietta College. Built ten years later, Erwin Hall (500 Putnam Street) is the oldest academic building still standing on the campus. It was named after Cornelius B. Erwin, a Connecticut industrialist who made a large donation to the college, despite never having seen it.

There are also many interesting homes and other buildings in Marietta, a number of which date back more than 150 years. Built in 1822 for postmaster H.P. Wilcox and latter occupied by Colonel John Mills, a founder of Marietta College, the Wilcox-Mills House (301 5th Street) has served as the college president's home since 1937. It is a Federal-style brick residence with an adjoining carriage house.

There are two Bosworth Houses of note in Marietta—one neglected, one not. The earliest was built in 1831 for Charles Bosworth (123 Maple Street).

He came to Marietta with his parents and siblings in 1816 and learned the boat building trade. In 1828, Charles with was widower with two daughters. After he remarried, he built this formidable two-story brick house while supporting his family as steamboat captain.

The newer Bosworth-Bisantz House (315 5th Street) was built in 1868 for Martin Pomeroy Wells, of the merchant firm Bosworth & Wells. In 1897, it was purchased by oilman Frank B. Bisantz, whose family lived in it for eighty-five years. The original red-brick structure was Victorian in design, but Bisantz added a Queen Anne tower and a wrap-around porch. Although it is owned by a preservationist group, its future still remains in doubt.

The Castle (418 4th Street) is a striking 1856 Gothic Revival home; this historic Victorian structure does, indeed, resemble a castle. Originally the site of the one of the earlies potteries in the Northwest Territory, the house was occupied by lawyers, bankers, land and oil speculators and a state senator. It now is operated as a museum.

Although founded in 1869, the First Unitarian Universalist Society of Marietta (232 3rd Street) occupies a Gothic Revival edifice constructed in 1858 for a Unitarian church. This followed the merger of the two denominations.

Originally a separate settlement, Harmar Village, founded in 1785 across the Muskingum River from downtown Marietta, was the first military installation in the Northwest Territory. It is connected to Marietta by the oldest operating swing bridge in the country. There are a number of historic structures within its compass. Among them are the David Putnam House (519 Fort Street), built in 1805, which served as both the home of the Putnam family and the first bank in Ohio, and the Levi Barber House (407 Fort Street), built by Congressman Levi Barber, which has been occupied by members of the Barber family since 1829.

There is also the two-story brick Henry Fearing House (131 Gilman Avenue), built by Henry in 1847. He was the son of Paul Fearing, a graduate of Harvard and the first lawyer in the Northwest Territory. Owned by the Washington County Historical Society, it purportedly exemplifies the lifestyle of a middle-class family during the Victorian era.

One of the most imposing homes in Harmar Village is the Anchorage (424 George Street)—a twenty-two-room, 1859 Italianate villa built by Douglas Putnam for his wife, Eliza, three years before she died. Douglas was the great-grandson of General Israel Putnam. A sturdy sandstone edifice, it overlooks Harmar Village and is owned by the Washington County Historical Society.

Not to be overlooked are the Muskingum Waterway—the only remaining complete system of hand-operated locks in the United States—and the *W.P. Snyder Jr.*, the only intact, steam-driven sternwheel towboat still on the nation's river systems. Constructed in 1918, it is permanently moored on the Muskingum River at Sacra Via.

Chapter 4

WORTHINGTON, 1803

Franklin County

"New Englanders on the Frontier"

On May 5, 1802, representatives of eight families met at the home of Reverend Eber B. Clark in Granby, Connecticut, and formed the Scioto Company. Their purpose was to establish a settlement in the Ohio Country somewhere between the Muskingum and Great Miami Rivers. They chose James Kilbourne to be their leader. In August of the same year, Kilbourne and Nathaniel W. Little were welcomed at the home of Colonel Thomas Worthington in Chillicothe. Worthington was a pioneering landowner and future governor who would be instrumental in Ohio becoming a state in 1803.

While visiting with Colonel Worthington, Kilbourne purportedly created the first full map of Ohio by compiling the maps of different sections that Worthington kept in his office as register of the United States land office in Chillicothe. He and Little tentatively chose a tract of land along the Scioto River on the Pickaway Plains for their new settlement. However, according to historian Henry Howe, he did not make a purchase, fearing "that the State Constitution, then about to be formed, should tolerate SLAVERY, in which case the project would have been abandoned."[56]

Upon receiving word that the newly drafted constitution of Ohio prohibited slavery, the Scioto Company met again in Granby and decided to buy sixteen thousand acres thirty miles farther north from Dr. Jonas Stanbery and Jonathan Dayton, the latter an American Revolutionary War general. It was located along the Whetstone (now Olentangy) River and was part of

The Orange Johnson House Museum was the residence of Arora Buttles. *Authors' photo.*

the United States Military District, which had been divided into townships five miles square rather than the usual six.

Returning to Ohio the following May, Kilbourne conducted an inspection of the Ohio Company's purchase and was ecstatic. As he recorded in his journal, "We found Black Walnut, Hickory, Ash, Honey Locust, Hackberry, Whitewood, etc., which never grown [*sic*] on any but first rate land."[57] The rivers were as "clear, lively streams of pure water as ever flowed from a fountain."[58] Furthermore, "in one place I saw a thousand acres of the best clear meadow I ever saw in any place whatever."[59] He quickly hired seven workers to begin leveling the forest.

In August 1803, the company decided to name its settlement Worthington in honor of Thomas Worthington, who would go down in history as the "Father of Ohio Statehood." Perhaps more significantly, each member of the company agreed to contribute two dollars—about four days' wages—toward the creation of a subscription library.

The first settlers—mostly drawn from Hartford County, Connecticut, and Hampshire County, Massachusetts—departed for Ohio the next month. All except Ezra Griswold traveled by horseback. He chose to drive an oxcart and, consequently, was the first one to arrive at their new home. In addition to Worthington, other migrants from New England would establish Norwalk, Hudson, Granville, Hartford, Putnam and other Ohio towns. Therefore, most residents of these communities were "New Englanders on the Ohio frontier."[60]

However, the pioneers had been preceded by the Adena and Hopewell Indian cultures, as was evidenced by a large ceremonial mound, 20 feet tall and 192 feet in diameter. Located on what became Plesenton Drive, the Jeffers Hopewell Prehistoric Mound was originally part of a larger group of earthworks. Two Adena mounds and a related earthwork are preserved in Highbanks Metro Park about five miles north of Worthington.

Before the members of the Scioto Company came to Worthington, they had agreed to lay out their settlement following the New England model (i.e., a grid pattern with a village green in the center). Each family would own at least one lot in town and another in the country for farming. The church and the school were assigned double lots facing the green and rural lots to support their operation. As Mira Parsons noted, "The first tree felled for building purposes was used in the erection of a log cabin which served for both church and school house."[61]

Having divided Worthington in 160 0.75-acre city lots with a five-acre public green in the center of the village, the Scioto Company—now consisting of forty families—held an auction. Thirty-seven people bid from $53.00 to $0.25 per lot. Those who didn't bid were given their choice of what remained. Farm lots, ranging from 20 to 130 acres, also went under gavel. An 80-acre farm lot and a 20-acre wood lot were earmarked for the Episcopal church and Worthington Academy, a proposed school.

On January 28, 1805, after the establishment of the library, church and school—which reflected the importance they placed on these institutions—the Scioto Company was officially dissolved. Each of the families was now left to its own devices. Although the settlers of Worthington were white, there were people of color living among them as early as 1807. For instance, "Black Daniel" worked in Amos Maxfield's brickyard. However, the first African Americans to purchase their own home in the village were Henry and Dolly Turk (108 West New England Avenue) in 1856. They came from Virginia, where Henry had bought Dolly's freedom eighteen years before. Other Black families would also settle in Worthington.

In 1808, the Worthington Academy was officially incorporated by the Ohio legislature, and a brick building was erected on the northeast quadrant of the public square. The same year, James Kilbourne constructed a building to house a newspaper, the *Western Intelligencer*, at 679–81 High Street. Now known as the Kilbourne Commercial Building, it holds the distinction of being the oldest commercial building in the state to be in continuous use. Although Kilbourne started the newspaper, it was quickly taken over by Ezra Griswold. It also housed a survey office, retail store and the Worthington Hotel.

Three years later, Griswold, who was also a private banker, built a brick tavern north of Worthington Academy, and Arora Buttles built a six-room house in 1811. Five years later, Orange Johnson, a comb maker, purchased the Buttles place and added a Federal-style addition that still stands. Now known as the Orange Johnson House (956 High Street), it has been converted into a museum, restored and maintained by the Worthington Historical Society.

The Reformed Medical Institute—an early medical college—opened in December 1830. It was founded by Wooster Beach, an ardent opponent of many accepted medical practices of the times. He emphasized the use of natural remedies and called his school of thought "Eclectic Medicine." However, it came under a barrage of criticism from rival medical schools and finally closed in 1839 following accusations of grave robbing—not unfounded—that culminated in the so-called Resurrection War.[62] When that structure was finally torn down in 1873, it was replaced by a public school.

More than thirty Worthington properties—including the Jeffers Hopewell Mound, the Kilbourne Commercial Building and the Orange Johnson House—are listed in the National Register of Historic Places. Following are some of the most notable.

St. John's Episcopal Church (700 High Street). Erected in about 1827–31 on the lot originally earmarked for it by the Scioto Company, the church was led by James Kilbourne, an ordained deacon. It is the first Episcopal congregation established west of the Allegheny Mountains.

The Worthington Inn (High Street and New England Avenue). The original portion was constructed as a private residence in 1831 by Rennsselear W. Cowles, who had arrived in Worthington fifteen years earlier. In addition to being a merchant, he served as county commissioner and justice of the peace. Following Cowles's death in 1842, Thomas Fuller bought the property and expanded the building. He then sold it to Theodore Fuller in 1852. Fuller converted it into an inn called Bishop House. In 1868, the Lewis family purchased the inn and continued to operate it as the Union Hotel. However, following a fire in 1889, it was sold to George Van Loon, who renamed it Central House. After another fire in 1901, a third floor and mansard roof were added by George's son, Nicholas, as well as a Victorian façade. The building has retained much the same appearance, even after the hotel rooms were converted to condominiums in 2007.

The Snow House (41 West New England Avenue). Dating back to about 1815, this structure is typical of a Federal-style brick home. John Snow, the house's best-known owner, was a key figure in Worthington and Ohio Masonic history. He was master of the local lodge when it was constructed and likely held the earliest meetings in his home.

The New England Masonic Lodge (634 High Street). Built in 1820, this is the oldest Masonic Temple west of the Allegheny Mountains in continuous use. Many of the founders of Worthington were Masons, and this undoubtedly played a part in their strong bond.

The former Episcopal Rectory (50 West New England Avenue). Built in 1841–45 southeast of the village green in the Greek Revival style, this now houses the offices, doll museum and library of the Worthington Historical Society.

Sharon Township Hall (67 East Granville Road). Built in 1856 as the first graded public school in Worthington, this site also provided a meeting place for the Independent Order of Odd Fellows Lodge, which rented the second floor. Sometime during the 1870s, it was sold to the Sharon Township trustees, who converted it into the town hall. For many years, it was the center of political and social events in Worthington. However, it is now owned by the Episcopal Church.

Gilbert House (72 East Granville Road). Also known as the Travis Scott House, this modified "saltbox"-style dwelling was built sometime about 1820 on Main Street and later moved to its present location. During the 1840s, it was occupied by the Ezra Gilbert family and represents the type of house a common laborer would have lived in during the early nineteenth century.

The Skeele House (700 Hartford Street). Originally built during the 1830s, this braced-frame house faced Granville Road. However, it was turned to face Hartford Street during the early part of the twentieth century. Harriett Skeele bought the house during the Civil War while her husband, Captain John S. Skeele, was off fighting with the 113th Ohio Voluntary Infantry. Fortunately, he survived the war, and the couple enjoyed fifty-nine years together until his death in 1919.

Boarding House (25 Fox Lane). The central portion of this residence was built in 1814 by the Worthington Manufacturing Company to provide housing for single male employees. This was the site of not only an early sawmill but also "a series of shops producing woolen cloth, leather goods, iron products, pot and pearl ash."[63] Then during the Civil War, it became Camp Lyon, where the 46th Ohio Volunteer Infantry trained.

Mattoon-Woodrow House (72 East North Street). Also known as the Ladd-Mattoon House, this Federal-style brick home was built in the late 1830s for Ansel Mattoon at the southwest corner of High and North Streets. A blacksmith by trade, Mattoon also served as president of the Worthington Anti-Slavery Society. Naturally, there are rumors that it was an Underground Railroad station, but there's no hard evidence. By the mid 1850s, it was being occupied by Reverend Thomas Woodrow, minister of the Worthington Presbyterian Church.

Buttles-Pinney-Brown House (12 East Stafford Avenue). Built by Arora Buttles in 1818, this Federal-style brick home was owned in succession by Buttles, merchant Abner H. Pinney and grocer and barrel maker Sidney Brown. It is similar in appearance to the John Snow, Orange Johnson and Mattoon-Woodrow Houses.

Adams-Heath House (721 High Street). Dating back to 1817–18, this house is the oldest wooden home in Worthington still remaining. The original owner, Demas Adams, married a stepdaughter of James Kilbourne and operated a boardinghouse in conjunction with the Worthington Hotel, located on the second floor of the Kilbourne Commercial Block. Later, it was the residence of Reverend Uriah Heath, a Methodist minister, who started a tree planting business in the town square.

Ripley House (623 High Street). This brick house, painted white, was the birthplace of Roswell S. Ripley in 1823. When he was six years old, his family moved to New York. Eventually, Ripley joined the military and served in the Mexican-American War. He was then stationed in Charleston, South Carolina, where he met the woman he would marry. When the South seceded from the Union, Ripley chose to stay in Charleston. Ripley was in command of the artillery that fired on Fort Sumter in Charleston Harbor, marking the start of the Civil War. For his actions, he was promoted to brigadier general and became a hero of the Confederacy.

Wright House (174 East New England). Yet another Federal-style home, this one was built for the Potter Wright family in 1818 on the site of what later would be used for the Methodist church. Fortunately, it was moved in the 1920s, likely saving it from demolition. "Wright was a manufacturer of carding equipment associated with the Worthington Manufacturing Company."[64]

Dr. Longenecker Office Building (633–35 High Street). The Snow family built the original portion of this building in about 1833 as a drugstore. However, it was enlarged and remodeled in the early twentieth century. From 1917 to 1926, it served as the dental office of Dr. Longenecker.

Colonel James Kilbourne's grave is in the Worthington cemetery, marked by a stone. Prior to his death, he had the names of his family, including that of his second wife, Cynthia Goodale Kilbourne, chiseled into it. But as Henry Howe recorded, "She took exception to the cutting of her name upon a tombstone before her death and directed that her remains should not be interred there."[65] Instead, she was buried at Green Lawn Cemetery on the opposite side of Columbus.

Although Worthington proper was always accepting of Black residents, the suburb of Colonial Hills, established in 1938, had a deed restriction prohibiting them from residing there. In response, Worthington residents founded the Worthington Human Relations Counsel. Even though the neighborhood was annexed in the 1950s, the restriction was never officially removed. However, it was nullified by the Civil Rights Act of 1964.

Chapter 5

MOUNT PLEASANT, 1803

Jefferson County

"An Abolitionist Stronghold"

As early as the 1650s, Ann Austin and Mary Fisher, two Quaker missionaries, came to North America from Barbados. Arriving in the Massachusetts Bay Colony, they were immediately arrested and imprisoned for their beliefs, which were contrary to those of the colony's Puritan government. Suspected of being witches, they were stripped naked in public and closely examined by a detail of women and one man who had donned a dress. After serving five weeks in jail—during which an effort was made to starve them to death—the two women were deported back to Barbados. And yet Quakers would continue to come to America.

Founded in England in 1652 by George Fox, the Society of Friends—as the Quakers were officially called—believe that "Christ speaks directly to each human soul who seeks Him, spiritual life depends upon direct communion with Him; all men may find salvation and life in Him."[66] Like Martin Luther, John Calvin, Ulrich Zwingli and other dissenters from the established church, Fox's views were considered dangerous.

Although he would remain in England, Fox had conceived the idea of establishing a separate colony in the New World and had even visited North America. Despite there being members of the Friends among the earliest colonists who settled in Massachusetts, Maryland and Virginia, the Quakers soon discovered that there was little more tolerance for their beliefs in the New World than there had been in the Old. So they decided what they needed was a colony of their own.

The Elizabeth Gill Mansion Museum is in the heart of the historic district. *Authors' photo.*

In 1674, two Quakers—John Fenwick and Edward Billings—purchased half of New Jersey from Lord Berkeley. A few years later, Admiral William Penn secured a grant of land from King Charles II in consideration of "the debts due to him and his father from the Crown."[67] Penn's initial concern was to obtain freedom of religion for the Society of Friends, but he soon decided to open the colony of Pennsylvania to other faiths. As a result, immigrants began to pour in from Wales, England, Germany and the Netherlands.

Very quickly, the Quakers became dissatisfied with the form of government Penn had established, viewing it as too liberal. It also permitted slavery. The Society of Friends originally had no official position on slavery, and some were, in fact, slaveholders. Nevertheless, they were the first religious movement to formally condemn it. Furthermore, many of the Quakers in Pennsylvania and other slave states opted to move farther west to escape slavery and, in many instances, work in a peaceful way to abolish it.

As historian Harlow Lindley has noted, "Probably the greatest contributing factor in this movement was the slavery issue, and after the passage of the famous Ordinance of 1787, Friends knew that the territory north and west of the Ohio would be forever free from slavery."[68]

The first Quakers to settle in Ohio were the George Harlan family, who took up residence in Deerfield on the Little Miami River in 1795, the same year the Treaty of Greenville was signed. The treaty opened up the Ohio

Country to settlement without fear of Indian reprisals. Other Quakers soon followed. By 1800, an estimated eight hundred members of the church had arrived in what would become the state of Ohio. There was a wholesale migration of Quakers "with the removal of one entire meeting and part of another from North Carolina to the Short Creek region a few miles west of the Ohio River above Wheeling, [West] Virginia."[69] A meeting was an administrative unit of the Society of Friends, and there were from fifty to one hundred individuals in this group.

The Quakers were so impressed with their new homes in Jefferson and Belmont Counties that they urged other meetings to join them. Even though they had to endure the many hardships that accompany true frontier living, they were free to live their lives according to their beliefs. In less than a year, so many Friends had moved to the region that they had established two meetings—Concord and Short Creek. The former was five miles from the future site of Mount Pleasant and the latter but a mile.[70] This was an area that had once been inhabited by the Indigenous peoples known as the Adena culture but had been abandoned long before European Americans occupied it.

Robert Carothers, a former Presbyterian from Virginia, had purchased 640 acres of what was then Smithfield Township in 1800 for two dollars per acre from the federal government. A few years later, Thomas Jesse and his brother John, Quakers from North Carolina, subsequently bought 100 acres from Carothers. During the following years, they laid out the village of Mount Pleasant, originally called Jesse-Bobtown. They then sold off much of the property, mostly to other Quaker families.

According to Lindley, "Within a few years the thriving town became one of the leading business and industrial centers of eastern Ohio and commanded trade over territory of more than a hundred square miles."[71] Enoch Harris, Joseph Gill and John Hogg opened the first stores. "There soon developed a flouring mill, a woolen factory, a tannery, and one of the first and largest pork packing establishments of the state. The most extensive meat market and one of the largest woolen markets of the state were here."[72]

Jesse Thomas opened a saddle and harness shop at the west end of Union Street. In 1808, he built the first brick house in the settlement, close to his shop but just outside the village. A young Benjamin Lundy came to work for him as a journeyman saddler in 1811. Four years afterward, he would marry into Jesse's wife's family.

Just prior to 1814, Jesse sold one acre and donated another to the Quaker Ohio Yearly Meeting. "It was estimated by some that there were over two thousand people in attendance at this first Ohio Yearly Meeting in 1813; others said that there were closer to three thousand Quakers present."[73] By any measure, it was an impressive gathering for such a remote location.

Coming together under fairly primitive conditions, the Friends conducted their business, which included laying plans for the construction of a meetinghouse. Jacob Ong, a carpenter and cabinetmaker, was the main designer and builder of the Mount Pleasant Yearly Meeting House. He was one of a number of Quakers who was a veteran of the American Revolution, despite his belief in pacifism. Jesse Thomas, on the other hand, had forfeited property instead of joining the fight. Although simple in design, the meetinghouse is two stories high, ninety-two feet long and sixty feet wide and boasts brick walls twenty-eight inches thick at the foundation.

By the time the meetinghouse, the first west of the Allegheny Mountains, was completed, Jesse had also become the director of the newly created Bank of Mount Pleasant, successfully guiding it through the financial crisis of 1819. Three years earlier, he had platted the "'Jesse Thomas Addition' to the village of Mt. Pleasant, consisting of 4 lots on the East side of Market Street."[74]

The two denominations—Presbyterian and Quaker—were not dissimilar, particularly when it came to their stance on slavery. Both were vehemently against it and sought its abolition. As a result, Mount Pleasant and neighboring Quaker communities were a hotbed for the abolitionist movement and active in the Underground Railroad. Although other religions would be represented, the village of Mount Pleasant remained predominantly Quaker.

In 1817, Charles Osborn, a Quaker, established the *Philanthropist*, the first newspaper in the nation devoted to the abolition of slavery. Owing to Mount Pleasant's remote location, however, little came of it, and the name was later adopted by James Birney of Cincinnati for his antislavery newspaper. Just four years later, Benjamin Lundy picked up where Osborn left off, publishing the *Genius of Universal Emancipation*. From his home base in Mount Pleasant, he likewise argued for the abolition of slavery. Furthermore, Lundy opened a "free labor store" in which all of the goods were produced by free men, not slaves. He later relocated his newspaper to Baltimore, Maryland.

"By 1826," historians have noted, "more than eight thousand Quakers were peacefully living among the limestone hills of Belmont, Jefferson, Harrison, and Columbiana counties in the eastern part of the state. For nearly seventy-five years, one-third of the Friends in America lived within the boundaries of the Old Northwest Territory."[75] Another wave of settlement took place a decade later, led by Quakers with large families seeking land for their children.

The citizens of Mount Pleasant also stressed mental and spiritual development. "There were a number of college men among the early settlers and great interest was shown in the development of schools," Lindley related. "In 1837 there was erected the Friends Boarding School. This school did valuable service."[76] However, the main building was destroyed by fire in 1875, and the school was relocated to Barnesville, another Quaker community. Also in 1837, the first meeting on the abolition of slavery in Ohio convened in Mount Pleasant.

In 1840, John W. Gill built the first factory in the United States for the weaving of silk. Unfortunately, Ohio did not prove to have a suitable climate for such an enterprise. "Although the Quakers were small in number, relatively speaking, yet they made their impress upon the life of Ohio, particularly in the Counties of Jefferson, Columbiana, Belmont, Guernsey, Morgan, Washington, Ross, Highland, Clinton, Warren, Greene, Preble, Miami, Logan and Morrow."[77]

Because of their belief that they should draw apart from society, the Quakers adopted a uniform manner of dress: "The men were attired in black, broad-brimmed, and undented beaver hates and collarless coats; the women dressed in long full skirts, shawls, often of Quaker gray, and bonnets which framed their faces; children looked like miniature adults."[78] Another custom that set these "peculiar people" apart from many other Americans was their failure to observe Christmas. Quakers felt that every day should be regarded as Christmas. And their speech was characterized by the use of the pronouns "thee" and "thou." This would begin to change during World War II.

The Historical Society of Mount Pleasant owns six historically significant properties. Thirty other properties that speak to the history of Mount Pleasant also helped in securing the town's designation as a National Historic Landmark District. These include the Friends Meetinghouse, the center of the Quaker faith in Eastern Ohio. Annual meetings continued to be held there for nearly a century, ending in 1909.

The Benjamin Lundy House and adjoining Free Labor Store were built in 1812. Lundy was the person who recruited William Lloyd Garrison, a leading abolitionist, into the movement. The P.L. Bone Store is a hewn-log structure built in 1804 by Enoch Harris. John W. Gill/Elizabeth House Mansion Museum was built in 1835 by the son of town founder Joseph Gill. It illustrates how quickly the community had begun to prosper. The Tin Shop dates back to 1840 and represents one of the early tradesmen in the community. Built in 1895, the Burriss Store represents Mount Pleasant during a later stage in its development.

Other historical buildings are not generally accessible to the public, but they can be viewed from the outside. These include Quaker Hill, built by George Jenkins in 1807; a series of row houses built by Samuel Jones during 1814–15; tanner John Hogg's 1840 home; Jonathan Binns's 1856 Federal-style house; David Updegraff's 1858 Italianate house; Mapleview, a Victorian house from 1895; and Dr. Finley's 1889 Queen Anne house.

The homes of Jenkins, Binns, Hogg and Updegraff were all purportedly stops on the Underground Railroad and used to assist fugitives from slavery in making their escape to freedom. When asked if they were harboring slaves, Quakers could answer truthfully that they weren't because they believed that all men and women were free.

Not surprisingly, there were people of color who also settled in or near Mount Pleasant. Seven years after their marriage, the Walkers—a biracial couple—arrived in Mount Pleasant in 1850. Moses Walker, the father, worked as a barrel maker to support their family of five. They "were living at the foot of a hill in the shadow of a large Friends meeting house, and in the larger shadow cast by the town's outsized reputation for opposing slavery."[79] Yet they were only fifteen miles from the slave market of Wheeling, (West) Virginia.

Moses Walker had come to Ohio from Pennsylvania or possibly Virginia. He and his wife, Caroline, may have formerly been enslaved. Their son, Moses Fleetwood Walker, was born there in 1857 and went on to become the first of his race to play major-league baseball in the nineteenth century—more than a half century before Jackie Robinson. No doubt Walker's parents had moved to Mount Pleasant to seek respite from a society marked by racism. Moses Fleetwood attended Oberlin College and the University of Michigan and was responsible for several inventions.

Three years after Moses Fleetwood's birth, the Walkers moved twenty miles northeast to Steubenville. In this new community, the father became a doctor and a minister in the Methodist Episcopal Church. However, he also was actively promoting the purchase of land in Liberia for Black people in American to populate. He planned to call this colony Ohio. In 1908, Moses Fleetwood Walker published a book titled *Our Home Colony: A Treatise on the Past, Present, and Future of the Negro Race in America*. He had come to believe that whites and Blacks could never peacefully coexist in the United States, despite his own accomplishments.

Mount Pleasant's importance belies its size. Although it is no longer an abolitionist hotbed, Mount Pleasant remains frozen in time—an early nineteenth-century village nestled in the gentle hills of southeastern Ohio. But as the population continues to decline, its long-term prospects are concerning.

Chapter 6

GRANVILLE, 1805

Licking County

"Companies of Neighbors"

It's not by happenstance that Granville, Ohio, looks like a stereotypical New England town plopped down in the heartland of Ohio. That was the intent. After all, it was founded in 1805 by residents of Granville, Massachusetts, who were looking to make a new start. They didn't really want to pull up stakes and move west, but their options were limited. Then, just over a century later, Granville's citizens began to focus on making their village a model community while preserving their history. As a result, little has changed.

By the early 1800s, many New Englanders were faced with an economic crisis. The population was exploding, but the farms were played out. The soil was so exhausted from mismanagement that it could no longer support food production. Many of its citizens looked to the west in the hope that they would find prosperity there, especially in the newly formed state of Ohio. As Richard Shiels has pointed out:

> *Companies of neighbors from Connecticut settled both Norwalk and Hudson, Ohio. South of the Western Reserve most Ohio towns were settled by Americans from states south of New England, but Worthington was settled by a company of people from Granby, Connecticut, just two years before Granville was settled by people from neighboring Granville, Massachusetts.*[80]

The Buxton Inn is in the center of a complex of historic properties. *Authors' photo.*

Samuel Everett—who lived halfway between Granby, Connecticut, and Granville, Massachusetts—was the one who initiated the formation of the Licking Company, as it called itself, with the help and encouragement of the group that founded Worthington, Ohio. With 107 subscribers from Granville, Massachusetts, and neighboring Granby, Connecticut, they wound up buying twenty-nine thousand acres in Licking County, Ohio, for $48,000 (nearly $1.2 million in today's dollars).

The area they settled in was known as the "Military Lands," territory that the U.S. government had seized in the Northwest Indian War in the 1790s.[81] After driving the tribes out of Ohio, the federal government carved up the land it had seized and gave it to the Revolutionary War veterans as compensation for their service.[82] However, few veterans actually wanted the land, so speculators swooped in, buying their parcels for pennies on the dollar. They then bundled them up and offered them to those who were interested, such as the Licking Company. Lieutenant Levi Buttles of Worthington, who served as the president of the Licking Company, is thought to have chosen the site where Granville is located. But then he continued west in 1804 and was replaced by Timothy Rose.

In 1805, the Licking Company immediately dispatched three parties of men well ahead of the family groups. Perhaps a dozen went first to plant corn and clear as much land as they could. A second party, led by Timothy Spelman, followed for the purpose of building a gristmill and sawmill and, if time allowed, constructing some cabins. The third group, including James Coe, a surveyor, was then sent to map out the village and divide up the land in one-hundred-acre parcels. They brought with them a detailed plan that included a public square, school, library, churches and a cemetery.

Late in the year, some 150 settlers arrived in ox-drawn wagons, having undertaken the arduous trek through the Alleghenies even as winter was approaching. They immediately set about building temporary shelters on the public square. But they weren't entirely alone. Several Welsh families had arrived a year or two earlier, settling on two thousand acres to the east known as the Welsh Hills. And there were squatters as well who had to be evicted.

However, it was the abundance of ancient earthworks that attested to the existence of the mound building Hopewell culture more than five centuries earlier. They left behind the Newark Earthworks, the largest geometric earthworks in the world. But in what would become Granville proper, there is a large effigy mound in the shape of a four-footed animal with a round head and a long tail. Called the Alligator Mound (at the end of Byrn Du Drive), it is more likely a depiction of an opossum or a panther. Most recent research suggests that it was built by the Fort Ancient tradition, which followed the Hopewell.

Granville was, according to Lisska et al. in their three-volume history of the community, a hybrid of the historic New England town and the uniquely midwestern township. "The founders immediately laid out their town not by the template of the typical New England village with its meandering lanes descended from Old World experience, but according to the grid suggested by the Northwest Ordinance of 1787."[83] Nestled among three hills that define its limits, it is reached by two wide roads that converge at the town square. On each of its four corners is a church—all Protestant.

To a large extent, the town plats of Worthington and Granville are nearly identical, except that the former had sixteen city blocks and the latter twenty-four. They also have similar village greens. It was historian William Utter's belief that either Granville copied Worthington or that they were both following a common New England model. "From the onset there was little about Granville that was haphazard," Utter observed. "The streets pointed directly to the compass bearings; houses and barns were aligned with the streets."[84] For some Worthington residents such as Captain Job Case, Granville proved to be so attractive that he moved there shortly after its founding, while still maintaining his property in Worthington.

A log schoolhouse was the first public building erected in Granville. In 1809, it was replaced by a frame building that also served as the meetinghouse for the Congregational Church. "In accordance with the best tradition of New England migration," Utter wrote, "a congregation was formally organized, well in advance of the exodus."[85] However, only twenty-seven members belonged to that denomination.

The oldest surviving structure in Granville is the home of Elias Gillman, who led the first family party to Ohio. Known as the "Wee White House," it was built in 1808 and later became the nucleus of the Kappa Alpha Theta sorority house (200 North Mulberry Street). The frame building also served as a post office, library, retail store and school. The local chapter of the Woman's Christian Temperance Union was organized there during the 1880s.

The intent was for Granville to be self-sufficient. From the beginning, it was a place of commerce and manufacture, most notably the Granville Furnace, which produced a popular cast-iron stove. During its first twenty-five years, Granville was home to eleven water-powered mills for grinding corn, milling flour, sawing lumber and producing woolen textiles. There were also numerous distilleries and cider presses, as well as "tanners, brickmakers, milliners, shoemakers, furniture builders, quarrymen and stone dressers."[86]

To facilitate all of this trade, the first bank opened in 1815, and a general store and an inn soon followed. However, when both the National Road and the Ohio & Erie Canal bypassed the village in the 1830s, its industries died off. As a result, it is now known primarily as the home of Denison University, a private liberal arts college founded in 1831 as the Granville Literary and Theological Institution. As the college grew, so did Granville.

The priority placed on education led to the establishment of five schools altogether, for both males and females. They reflected the Puritan moral code. As abolitionism began to spread across the country, a division arose within the Christian churches. This culminated in the Granville Riot of 1836, when an abolitionist convention was held in Granville against the wishes of the mayor and seventy other leading citizens. This led to a clash between a gang of local troublemakers, supplemented by outside agitators, and convention delegates.[87]

Although Granville was not on one of the primary Underground Railroad routes, the antislavery cause had more supporters following the riot, and some citizens became involved in aiding fugitives from slavery. In one local case, a runaway from Kentucky known only as "John" was captured on his way from Newark to Granville. A hearing was held in the Conference Room of the Congregational Church before a capacity crowd. Despite the fact that John's owner had the necessary paperwork to support his claim, Judge Samuel Bancroft ruled that the arrest warrant was defective and immediately freed him.

During the Civil War, Granville was solidly Republican, except for a handful of Peace Democrats and "Copperheads." Despite a Confederate recruiting officer sneaking into Licking County, six hundred of its men marched off to join the Union army. As a result, there was a drastic drop in enrollment at Denison University that nearly led to its demise.

Once the soldiers returned, the college and the farms began to prosper again, and the village of Granville experienced an uptick in its growth. Because of the many visitors, a new hotel was needed. The village's "old time hotel"—the Mansion House—was razed, and the "Hotel Granville" was erected in its place. This three-story building could accommodate one hundred guests. On September 1, 1890, the first interurban line in the country made its inaugural trip between Newark and Granville. It was almost immediately awarded a contract to carry the U.S. mail between the two towns.

With the dawning of the twentieth century, the village elders decided that it was time to undertake some long-delayed civic projects. In 1906, they erected a municipal building with offices for the mayor and council, as well as a new jail. They also turned their attention to paving the village roads, after the main street had been "described as the worst piece of road between Columbus and Zanesville."[88]

In the first century of its existence, Granville acquired many impressive buildings and homes, many of which still stand. More than one hundred of them are listed in the National Register of Historic Places. For example, the commercial buildings that line East Broadway were built during the period of 1830–80. Among the most notable structures in the village is the Buxton Inn (313 East Broadway). Named after Major Horton Buxton, this tavern has been providing food and lodging continuously since 1812. A Federal-style building, it was once an overnight stop for stagecoaches. Visitors have included President Abraham Lincoln and author Harriet Beecher Stowe.

William Stedman built the Bank of the Alexandrian Society (115 East Broadway) in 1816. After the bank failed, the stone building housed a store, post office, library, restaurant and even an interurban depot. It now houses the Granville Historical Society Museum.

Denison University has offices in the Rose House (637 North Pearl Street), built in 1820 for Captain Levi Rose, a veteran of the War of 1812. It is an impressive brick dwelling in the Federal style. David Messenger's Tavern, later known as the Willard Warner House (303 East Broadway), was built three years later. Warner was a Civil War veteran who was later elected to the U.S. Senate. The building is currently used by the Buxton Inn as guest rooms.

Constructed in the Federal style, the Lucius Mower House (233 East Broadway) dates back to 1824. Mower was a merchant, financier and master craftsman who backed the Ohio and Erie Canals. After his death, the house was used as a bank by the Alexandrian Society.

The Henry L. Bancroft House (133 Prospect Street)—a two-story Victorian home in the Italianate style—was built by a local merchant, banker and carpenter. After inheriting a chest of carpenter's tools, he purportedly responded, "With this I was carve my fortune. I shall marry me a good wife; build me a good house and for ten years save one hundred dollars each year."[89]

In 1834, abolitionist Ashley A. Bancroft built a house (555 North Pearl Street) with stone quarried from the hillside behind it. Bancroft hosted the first convention of the Ohio Anti-Slavery Society two years later in his barn. Although there was little Underground Railroad traffic through Granville, Bancroft's son, Hubert, later wrote a firsthand account of his memories of it. The house now serves as a student residence for Denison University.

Bushnell House (337 West Broadway) was built in 1835–36 for Deacon Leonard Bushnell. "In 1836 the home was only half-finished and a fiery abolitionist, Theodore Weld, was coming to town. Deacon Bushnell had Weld speak on the second floor of his home, rather than in the church—he guessed correctly there would be eggthrowing, and figured his unfinished home wouldn't be damaged by the action."[90]

St. Luke's Episcopal Church (107 East Broadway) was constructed in 1837. The church was designed by Benjamin Morgan, an architect who was also working on the state capitol building in Columbus at the time. The Greek Revival–style building has changed very little over the intervening years.

The twenty-seven-room Greek Revival–style Avery-Downer House (221 East Broadway) was built in 1842 and expanded in 1873. It served as a fraternity house for the first half of the twentieth century, after which it was purchased by Robbins Hunter Jr. and is now a museum.

Dating back to 1855 or so, the "Castle" (323 Summit Street) is a wood-frame, one-story, Gothic Revival structure with crenellate battlements and square towners. It was built by Wallace Carpenter, purportedly for his wife, because he had promised her a castle, but this was all he could afford.

There are many more historically significant structures. However, coal and transportation tycoon John Sutphin Jones was associated with three of Granville's most impressive buildings. First he acquired the residence of Dr. Alfred Follett in 1896 when he married Follett's daughter and

The Granville Inn remains a popular venue for celebrations of all types. *Authors' photo.*

named it Monomoy Place (204 West Broadway). In 1905, Jones bought and renovated Bryn Du Mansion (537 Jones Road NE), a fifty-two-room Federal-style home that sits on a large estate on the edge of town that includes a polo field. And in 1924, he erected the Jacobean Revival–style Granville Inn (314 East Broadway), which continues to operate as a restaurant and hotel.

Chapter 7

RIPLEY, 1812

Brown County

"The Underground Railroad Town"

Ripley, about fifty miles southeast of Cincinnati on the Ohio River, was founded by Colonel James Poage (or Poague). A slave owner from Virginia by way of Kentucky, Colonel Poage came to abhor slavery. As a veteran of the American Revolution, he was granted land in the Virginia Military District, a region of Ohio that was specifically set aside for veterans by the government.

In 1804, Poage took his family and twenty slaves, whom he subsequently freed, and settled on one thousand acres of "Survey No. 418 in Ohio, along the Ohio River…and here he made his home and [in 1812] laid out a town, which he named Staunton, for Staunton in Virginia."[91] However, Poage wasn't the first slaveholder to do so.

According to historian Charles Galbreath, "As early as 1796, William Dunlop left Fayette County, Kentucky, and settled in Brown County, Ohio (then in the Northwest Territory)."[92] He also brought a large number of slaves with him, set them free and helped them settle on land in the vicinity of what would become Staunton.

Similarly, Dr. Alexander Campbell, a native of Virginia, was a physician in Cynthiana, Kentucky. After serving in the Kentucky General Assembly, he "removed to Ripley, Ohio, in 1803, taking with him several slaves and giving them their freedom."[93]

Brown County was also home to two large "Negro settlements" in Eagle and Scott Townships comprising the former slaves of Samuel Gist. When

The "House with 3 Doors" (center) is just one of many historic homes in Ripley. *Authors' photo.*

Gist died in 1815, his "will stipulated that within one year, his slaves would be freed and his property in America sold in order to provide for them and their heirs forever."[94]

Staunton was renamed Ripley in 1816 after General Eleazar Wheelock Ripley, who served in the War of 1812. Although it wasn't exactly planned in the usual sense, many like-minded individuals—opponents of slavery—were increasingly attracted or even recruited to the region.

Reverend Samuel Doak of Tennessee, a Princeton graduate, was one of them. Originally from Virginia, he inculcated his beliefs in many of the young men he trained for the ministry, including John Rankin, who married Jean Lowery, one of Doak's granddaughters. "However, it wasn't until about 1818 that the 'Presbyterian bishop,' as he was called, finally freed his own slaves. Eleven of them relocated to Brown County."[95]

Owing to its location on the Ohio River just across from Kentucky, Ripley quickly became one of the major crossing points for fugitives from slavery.[96] It didn't take long before Black and white residents, working together and separately, began aiding them in their escape to freedom. During the years leading up to the Civil War, the town became the home of many prominent abolitionists, as well as a haven for runaway slaves.

John Rankin arrived in 1822 and was installed as pastor of the Presbyterian church. Initially, he lived in a house in the town proper, but he later built one high on a hillside, some three hundred feet above Ripley, where he had a good view of the Ohio River. As one historian wrote, "At a window from dark to daybreak was ever the beacon light, easily seen from the Kentucky hills and the river bank, to which star of hope the fugitive's eye rested with delight—once here all was safe."[97] Reverend Rankin, his wife and his family aided hundreds, if not thousands of men, women and children on their flight from slavery.

Meanwhile, John P. Parker also was helping runaway slaves, some of whom he had actually gone to Kentucky to personally rescue. Concerning his own years in bondage, Parker said, "As a slave, all I knew was my father was one of the aristocrats of Virginia. Whoever he was, he gave me a brain which was a source of comfort even in my period of despair. He gave me one more advantage: the power to hate."[98]

Through hard work and frugality, Parker was able to purchase his freedom after eighteen years, becoming a free man in 1845. Four years later, after taking a wife, he settled in Ripley, where the local abolitionist society had three hundred members. By day, Parker ran an iron foundry, a notable accomplishment in itself. But by night he ferried countless runaways across the Ohio River.

"For nearly fifteen years, John P. Parker rescued fugitive slaves, leading the *Cincinnati Commercial Tribune* to write shortly after Parker's death, 'a more fearless creature never lived. He gloried in danger….He would go boldly over into the enemy's camp and filch the fugitives to freedom.'"[99]

Historian Ann Hagedorn told the story of Ripley's Underground Railroad in her book *Beyond the River*:

> *For the Rankin boys, and their father, for the father of Jimmy Campbell, Ripley's mayor, and for several other Front Street dwellers, 1838 would be a striking year….They were the men and women attuned to the traffic that picked up, rather than ceased, when the river froze: the human traffic of runaway slaves. For, somewhere on the other side of the river, on any given night, a slave, driven by the fear of capture, torture, and an endless future of bondage, was crossing a snowy field, wadding an icy stream, dodging men and dogs to reach a river he or she had only heard of but never see, to escape to the freedom beyond it.*[100]

There is no question that the borders of Ohio saw the highest Underground Railroad traffic. The operation of the Underground Railroad in Brown County so angered the slaveholders of Kentucky that they offered rewards for the assassination of Rankin, Campbell and others. One of them, Reverend John B. Mahan, was indicted in a Kentucky court for "aiding and assisting certain slaves" in their escape.[101] He spent nearly ten weeks in a Kentucky prison before he was released.

The sons of Nathaniel Collins, Theodore and Thomas, were also involved in the Underground Railroad, working hand in hand with the Rankin boys at times. Theodore made coffins in his workshop and frequently used them to transport runaways.

Dr. Isaac Beck was a founder of Sardinia. "Among those he worked with were the Pettijohns, a clan of twelve households, all of whom were Presbyterian and active in the Underground Railroad, and the families of Robert and William Huggins, who had settled first in Ripley then moved to Red Oak."[102] Hudson, a Black man who had been emancipated by Samuel Gist, was hired by Beck, Mahan and the Pettijohn brothers to smuggle fugitives from slavery at twenty-five cents apiece. As a result, both Beck and Mahan felt he had guided more fugitives to freedom than anyone else they knew.

An 1892 letter from Richard Rankin, John's son, to Professor Wilbur Siebert, an early chronicler of the Underground Railroad, provides a rare insight into the need to change plans on a moment's notice. Eleven slaves had escaped from Washington, Kentucky, in 1844, led by the free Black husband of one of them, Peter Dent. A reward of $2,200 was posted, and slavecatchers scoured Ripley and the surrounding countryside. Rankin stayed with the refugees throughout their passage through Brown County:

> *We were compelled to run them from William Minnow's to Aunt Mary Pogue's. When the pursuers came to Pogue's, we would run them to Washington Campbell's, from there to James McCoy's, and from James's to William McCoy's, thence to Kirby Bill Baird's, and thence back to Aunt Mary Pogue's, thence to Minnow's and across the woods to Campbell's, and so on.*[103]

Today, Ripley is regarded as the best-preserved example of a pre–Civil War Ohio River town in the state. Its fifty-five-acre historic district offers an amazing collection of historic buildings dating back to not long after the town was platted. For example, a series of row houses (110–104 North Front Street) still stands; they were built by Colonel James Poage, the town's founder, sometime prior to his death in 1820. Originally, they were shop fronts in the commercial district of Ripley. Known for his antislavery views,

Poage was undoubtedly responsible for attracting other abolitionists to Ripley. Poage himself lived in 128 North Front Street. His office was in the house to the left and the home of his daughter on the right.

When Reverend Rankin first arrived, he lived in a row of brick apartments (224, 222, 220 North Front Street) looking out over the Ohio River. It is likely that the alley on the right side of the building was used as an escape route by more than one fugitive from slavery once he or she set foot on the Ohio shore. Rankin did not have a high opinion of Ripley when he settled there, deeming it an "exceedingly immoral" place.[104] He had come from Tennessee, feeling that he could no longer abide living in a slave state. But if he was looking for sinners to minister to, it was perfect. Once he moved to his home on the hilltop, his Underground Railroad efforts began in earnest. "The entire family—wife, Jean, and children—helped care for the needs and provided transport for the fugitive slaves," historian Tom Calarco has written.[105] Up to as many as a dozen fugitives were provided a safe haven at one time, with the assistance of his nine sons.

The Rankin-McNishe House was a three-story structure built by Rankin in 1823 and later occupied by his in-laws, William and Lucinda McNishe. Rankin next built a small, red brick home (6152 Rankin Hill Road) in 1828 that sits at the very top of three hundred stone steps. Many fleeing slaves knew that food, clothing and rest awaited them at Rankin's house, and then they would be transported to the next station on the Underground Railroad.

One of the most impressive residences (114 North Front Street) on Ripley's River Walk is the two-story, white brick home of Dr. Alexander Campbell, a physician, merchant and, likely, Ohio's first abolitionist. Arriving in Ripley in 1803–4, his involvement in the Underground Railroad predated Rankin's and Parker's. He also served as a U.S. senator from 1809 to 1813. However, when the British burned Washington, he rode out of the city and never returned.

While a member of the Kentucky General Assembly, Campbell was in favor of a proposed constitution that would have banned slavery. When it failed, he moved to Ohio, but his native state didn't forget him, placing a $2,500 reward on his head for his capture or assassination. A similar reward was offered for Rankin, Mahan and Dr. Isaac Beck, who lived close by in Sardinia.

Carey Alexander Campbell, son of Senator Campbell, owned an 1837 Federal-style home (226 North Front Street). However, the Victorian porches and decorative trim were added in 1897. The Thomas McCague house (208 North Front Street) figured in an incident involving John Parker. Once at the break of dawn, Parker brought a part of fugitives to McCague's home while being pursued by slavecatchers. McCague purportedly called to Parker, "It's daylight, don't stop." However, his wife, Kitty, said, "Daylight or not daylight, Parker, bring them in."[106] A cabinetmaker by trade, McCague sometimes hid a few slaves in empty coffins on Parker's behalf. He also owned a pork packing plant and a flour mill and had his hand in banking.

The comparatively modest Kirker House (206 Front Street) was the home of Thomas Kirker. While attending Whitmore, a private school, future U.S. president Ulysses S. Grant boarded in this home. The school was later renamed Ripley College. Cabinetmaker Thomas Collins resided in a nearby Federal-style house (204 North Front Street) while also serving as a conductor on the Underground Railroad. He purportedly worked in concert with John Rankin.

At the corner of Mulberry and 2nd Streets is the Baird House (201 North 2nd Street). Built in 1825, it was occupied by three generations of the Baird family from 1845 to 1973. The most prominent family member was Chambers Baird Jr., an attorney and the editor of the *Ripley Bee*. His father, also an attorney, participated in two Underground Railroad legal cases. The first was *Mahan v. The Commonwealth of Kentucky* (1838), in which Reverend John B. Mahan was charged with aiding to fugitive slaves who had escaped into Ohio. The second involved a free Black family of five, the Hensleys, who were abducted from their home in Brown County in 1853 and transported to Kentucky.

Both Rankin and Mahan were well acquainted with Cincinnati's Levi Coffin, the so-called president of the Underground Railroad. Coffin ran his own loosely organized network out of Hamilton County and occasionally worked in concert with the Underground Railroad agents of Brown County. However, nearly every rescue was made up on the fly. There was danger is using the same plan repeatedly. The alleged Underground Railroad routes were subject to constant revision.

Five miles north of Ripley is the village of Red Oak. It is the site of one of the oldest Presbyterian congregations in Ohio, dating back to 1798; a fine old stone church, built in 1817; and a historic cemetery. For thirty-nine years, Reverend James Gilliland, who helped establish the Underground Railroad in southern Ohio, served as its pastor. "Gilliland and his congregation formed the core of the largest concentration of Underground Railroad conductors in Ohio."[107] He would become known as the "Apostle of Freedom."

In all, nearly thirty sites associated with the Underground Railroad have been identified and catalogued by Dewey Scott, docent at the John P. Parker

Few Underground Railroad conductors were as daring as Robert P. Parker. *Authors' photo.*

House (300 North Front Street) and a walking encyclopedia. Any trip to Ripley should begin at the Parker House; then work north to the Rankin House and finish up at Red Oak Presbyterian Church.

However, Ripley's population peaked in 1970 at 2,745—30 more people than lived there in 1860 at the heyday of the Underground Railroad. Like many small towns in Ohio, it is now struggling to remain relevant.

Chapter 8

GERMAN VILLAGE, 1814

Columbus, Franklin County

"Largest Private Undertaking in the World of Its Kind"

When Columbus was selected as the state capital in 1812, it didn't exist except on paper. Other places in contention did, including the towns of Chillicothe, Zanesville, Dublin, Worthington, Delaware and Franklinton. But an undeveloped spot on the "High Banks opposite Franklinton at the Forks of the Scioto known as Wolf's Ridge" won out because of its central location and access to transportation routes (namely the river and a muddy road), not to mention the fact that four Franklinton business owners offered to donate some land.[108] The land would be used for a statehouse—and a prison. Ohio badly needed both, the prison possibly more so.

As a result, Columbus was a planned community without a plan, or at least not much of one. As it turned out, Franklinton wasn't much of a place either, judging by Judge Gustavus Swan's description. "When I opened my office in Franklinton in 1811," he observed, "there was neither church, nor schoolhouse, nor pleasure carriage in the county, nor was there a bridge over any stream within the compass of an hundred miles….I feel safe in asserting that there was not in the county a chair for every two persons, nor a knife and fork for every four."[109] It wasn't surprising, then, that it was also passed over for the honor of being the state capital. And it was a good choice, given that much of Franklinton—also known as "the Bottoms"—would subsequently be underwater a century later during the Great Flood of 1913.

A typical street scene in historic German Village. *Authors' photo.*

Wolf's Ridge was part of the Refugee Tract. This particular piece of land had been set aside for Nova Scotians who had supported the colonists during the American Revolution. Few if any had moved there, and it sat largely empty. So a town was platted that "ran from North Public Lane (Nationwide Boulevard) to South Public Lane (Livingston Avenue) and from the river to East Public Lane (Parsons Avenue)."[110] Of course, the city's planners kept some key tracts for themselves.

Mound Street, just south of Main, was named by surveyor Joel Wright because there was a forty-foot-tall Indian mound right where it intersected with what became High Street. Three hundred feet in diameter with a thicket of trees growing from it, the mound was left relatively unmolested for many years, other than a house being built atop it by one Dr. Young. High Street simply jogged around it. But during the 1830s, it was leveled and the clay used to make bricks.

Between 1812 and 1816, when the capital was actually moved to Columbus from Chillicothe, a lot of work had to be done. According to the Ohio History Connection:

> *By 1813, a penitentiary had been built, and by the following year the first church, school, and newspaper had been established. The* [original] *statehouse was built in 1814 as well. Columbus grew quickly in its first few years, having a population of seven hundred people by 1815. It officially became the county seat in 1824. By 1834, the population of Columbus was four thousand people, officially elevating it to "city status."*[111]

However, other than the Ohio Statehouse—the second one, actually—little remains of pioneering Columbus, at least in the downtown. But just south of Livingston Avenue is German Village, at 233 acres the largest privately funded preservation district in the National Register of Historic Places.[112] Although the architecture owed little to their German origins, the people brought much of their culture with them.

When the U.S. Congress appropriated Refugee Lands in 1796 for those veterans who had supported the winning side in the American Revolution, John McGowan claimed 328 acres. He didn't really want to live here, but as German immigrants began arriving in central Ohio, McGowan sold tracts of land in what came to be called "die alte sud ende" (the old south end). By 1814, this area had become a German colony, with some of the immigrants hired to work on the first statehouse, which saw construction begin in 1839.

By 1850, nearly half of Ohio's immigrants had come from the German lands. More than 90 percent of them were peasants who had endured serfdom, a type of forced labor. Many had fled the German revolutions of 1848–49 following the collapse of the Holy Roman Empire. As the local German-language newspaper, *Der Westbote*, noted in 1855, "The people who live in these small houses work very hard. You will not find silver on the doors, but you will find many little gardens which produce vegetables for the city's market. You will not find silk or other very expensive things; but the houses are very clean, the people work hard, and are very healthy, and they are very happy."[113] And their schools were so superior to the English-speaking ones that many non-German children were sent to them.

In May 1855, the forty-member Turnverein, a German social group that stressed physical fitness, marched through the streets of Columbus on its way to Stewart's Grove for a picnic. As historian Alfred Lee recounted, "During the parade the society's colorbearer carried a red silk flag bordered in black and inscribed with mottoes in yellow German letters."[114] A malicious rumor soon spread that the banner was the "Red Republican Flag of Germany" and that it was inscribed with words hostile to American institutions.

It didn't take long for the adherents of the anti-immigrant Know Nothing Party to gather. They confronted the Turners that evening at the canal bridge near Friend Street and demanded the flag be lowered. When the Germans refused, one of the Know Nothings tried to seize the flag by force. A scuffle ensued, the banner was ripped and several people were injured. During the course of the evening, additional disturbances broke out. The rowdies then began throwing stones, and some of the Turners were severely beaten by the mob. It was later determined that the offending language on the flag read "Blithe, Merry and Free" on one side and on the opposite "Through exercise, strength; through investigation, knowledge. Freedom."[115]

Similar conflict would occur in July between the Turnverein and the Know Nothings, with more rock throwing and even some exchange of gunfire. There was no doubt the Turners were provoked. One young man was killed, whether by accident or on purpose is not known. Some nineteen Germans—"many of whom were undoubtedly innocent"—were arrested in the confusion and hauled off to jail.[116] Those who were eligible to vote were then forced to issue a denial that they had voted in favor of the Kansas-Nebraska Act (which allowed new states to choose whether they wanted to be slave or free) and had voted for the Republican ticket. As far as the person responsible for the death of the fifteen-year-old boy, there was no agreement.

As of 1865, one-third of the city's population was German. They built their homes and businesses in an area bounded by City Park (which became Stewart's Grove), 3rd Street and Livingston Avenue. Because there were no zoning laws, the two types of buildings were intermixed. Often a businessman and his family would live above the business. Stewart's Grove was renamed Schiller Park in 1891 in honor of Frederick Schiller, the German poet.

The businesses that were established in German Village catered to the needs and desires of the German people. As a result, there were many churches, newspapers, breweries, bakeries and sausage-making shops. The Germans established a handful of singing societies and athletic clubs that helped to reinforce their sense of community and ethnic pride. In 1838, Louisa Frankenberg started what is often cited as the first kindergarten—"children's garden"—in America, which she would operate for many years. During the same period, the Lutheran Theological Seminary was founded, which later gave birth to Capital University.

One Columbus-born German American, George J. Karb, a druggist, would be elected mayor in 1890, as well as police commissioner, city council member and sheriff of Franklin County. He would serve as mayor again during World War I. Karb's popularity was such that he served nine times as an elected official. To illustrate the impact of the German immigrants on Columbus, in 1907–8 the public schools had 94 high school teachers, 446 elementary school teachers and 18 special German teachers for a total of 558. And they desperately needed more German teachers.

German Village was a thriving Columbus neighborhood. But then World War I broke out. Like much of the United States, Columbus was swept by strong anti-German sentiment. This led to demonstrations in which German books were burned and German dog breeds such as German Shepherds and Dachshunds were slaughtered. In addition, German-language newspapers were pressured to close, and the speaking and teaching of German was forbidden. Locally, city officials "renamed Schiller, Germania, Kaiser, and Bismarck streets as Whittier, Stewart, Lear, and Lansing Streets. Schiller Park became Washington Park."[117] Later, the Schiller name was reinstated along with a bronze statue of the poet.

When Prohibition (1920–33) was enacted, the German Village breweries closed, and the German workers had to seek jobs elsewhere. Many of them began moving into the newly developed suburbs. This would only increase after World War II, resulting in an overall decline in the quality of life in the neighborhood. By the early 1960s, most properties had become rentals, and urban renewal became a distinct possibility. And if the city fathers had had their way, German Village would have been leveled.

However, Frank Fetch felt otherwise. He had been living in German Village since 1949 and believed that the decaying neighborhood could be revitalized. Although the area from Main Street south to Livingston Avenue was declared "blighted" and was condemned by the city, Fetch rallied his neighbors to ensure that the wholesale demolition stopped where German Village began. This resulted in the founding of the German Village Society, whose mission was to save and restore this historic area.

German Village may not have been a planned community when it started, but it is now. Since 1960, the German Village Commission has worked to ensure that any exterior alterations of properties located within the boundaries of the historic district adhere to its mission "to preserve, protect, and enhance the unique architectural and historical features" of the village.[118]

Most of the buildings still standing in German Village were constructed from 1850 to 1910. The very characteristics that apply to "blighted" areas are what give German Village its unique charm: "small lots, narrow streets and the absence of new development."[119] And it was accomplished without government programs or subsidies.

Since 1960, more than 1,600 buildings have been restored. In the process, German Village became a model of urban neighborhood preservation and revitalization. And it has become a highly desired (i.e., pricey) area in which to live. It is where novelist Sue Grafton, author of the "Alphabet Series" featuring private investigator Kinsey Millhone, lived and worked while her husband attended Ohio State University.[120]

Although German Village is best appreciated as a whole, there are places that deserve special attention. Take the so-called Schwartz's Castle (492

South 3rd Street). Built by pharmacist Dr. Frederick William Schwartz in 1880, this towering brick structure has inspired a handful of legends, but there is little truth in any of them. Schwartz was eccentric for the times, but he was not the mystical madman many believed him to be. He was simply fanatical about his health—a vegetarian who believed in taking walks, barefoot, and sun baths, sans clothing.

3rd Street is the main north–south artery bisecting German Village. It runs from Schiller Park to Livingston Avenue and is lined by many residential and commercial buildings. Many retail shops and dining establishments are located along it or nearby on intersecting streets.

The recently restored St. Mary of the Assumption Catholic Church (684 South 3rd Street) is the crown jewel of German Village. Completed in 1868, this brick edifice features an impressive spire that also has a clock on each side and a forty-eight-bell carillon. With its painted ceilings and magnificent stained-glass windows, Grand Old St. Mary's was chosen as the best religious venue in the city in 2022.

Built by Amelia Maurer in 1887, the main part of the thirty-two-room rabbit warren known as the Book Loft (631 South 3rd Street) was originally Maurer's Saloon. However, the arrival of Prohibition in 1919 resulted in its being repurposed for everything from a theater and a church to a doll hospital and an indoor golf course. It finally found its true calling in 1977 when it opened as one of the largest independent bookstores in the country. The *New York Times* has called the Book Loft "a national treasure."

Nothing says German Village like Schmidt's Sausage Haus (240 East Kossuth Street). Upon its opening in 1886, it was known as J. Fred Schmidt Meat Packing House. The Schmidt family immigrated to Columbus in the early 1880s from Frankfurt, Germany. Their first venture into the restaurant business came when Fred's son George opened a stand at the Ohio State Fair in 1914, and it continues to this day. But in 1967, Fred's grandson George opened their first restaurant in the shadow of the packing plant. It has since became a landmark, known for its German cuisine, including Bahama Mamas and cream puffs.

In 1884, a two-story brick building opened its doors as Daeumler's Grocery (169 East Beck Street). However, it soon became a saloon, operating under a variety of names: Daeumler & Oldhausen, the Tide House Saloon and the King's Rose Garden. Unofficially, it was also known as the Bucket of Blood, one of several Columbus venues to bear that nickname. But the King's Rose had true bloodstains to show for it on its front steps. It later

Saint Mary of the Assumption Roman Catholic Church is a German Village landmark. *Nheyob/Wikipedia.*

became the Palmer House, The Lindenhof and, most recently, Lindey's, a fine dining establishment.

There are many beautiful houses surrounding Schiller Park, but Friedrich Wittenmeier's two-story brick dwelling (147 East Deshler Park) comes with a good story. Wittenmeier was a master stonemason who moved into contracting. However, because he lost his shirt (figuratively and perhaps literally) on the statehouse annex job in 1901, he also lost his house a dozen years later.

In truth, there is a story behind nearly every structure in German Village, which is why there are a half dozen or so books devoted to its history. It also is a flourishing community, although it is not particularly German or working class.

Chapter 9

ROSCOE VILLAGE, 1816

Coshocton County

"America's Canal Town"

When Europeans arrived in what would become Coshocton County, they found remnants of an earlier civilization left behind by the region's prehistoric inhabitants. There were earthworks, stone axes and flints, and just west of the future village of Roscoe, surveyor Andrew Fisher reported seeing "traces of a belt of red soil…thirty feet wide, encircling a hilltop. The circle was three hundred feet in diameter."[121]

Although it may have appeared to be wilderness, the site was well known to the Indigenous peoples, who traveled the so-called Cuyahoga-Muskingum Trail. According to historians Paul and Sally Misencik, "It stretched from the mouth of the Cuyahoga River at present Cleveland, Ohio, to the mouth of the Muskingum River at present Marietta, Ohio."[122] Along the way, it passed through the Moravian mission villages of Schoenbrunn, Goshen and Gnadenhütten, before crossing the Walhonding River at Roscoe.

In about 1809 or 1810, James Calder arrived in Coshocton and opened a country store. He was the settlement's first merchant, although Charles Williams had once kept a limited stock of dry goods at his tavern. But when Calder's business failed a half-dozen years later, he picked up and moved across the Muskingum River, to where he still owned a tract of land. Here he established a settlement he called Caldersburg. He would spend the rest of his life on a farm two miles outside of the village, making and selling wooden shingles.

Many of the original canal-era buildings are still being used in Roscoe Village. *Lexi Walker photo.*

Calder had laid out Caldersburg in January 1816, "partly in the narrow valley that skirts the river and partly on the steep bluff that rises just beyond."[123] The original plat consisted of sixty-seven lots in what would be the lower part of the town. At first, the only advantage that Caldersburg had over Coshocton was that the farmers did not have to pay twenty-five cents to cross the river by ferry to get to it.

One of Caldersburg's few attractions was the large log tavern of William Barcus, where an itinerant preacher sometimes would conduct a service—hymn, prayer and sermon—in the dining room. By 1821, Barcus had competition when Theophilus Phillips erected a brick tavern right across the street from him. Apparently, there was enough traffic to keep both of them in business.

Having put aside some money by making salt at three dollars per bushel, James LeRetilley opened a store in 1825 in partnership with William Wood and later George Bagnall. Bagnall had been Wood's partner in the salt business as well but were forced to close when competition heated up. As it turned out, there prospects would be brighter than they realized in just a few years.

In 1828, Jackson Township was organized and contained Caldersburg. But almost from the onset, the township split into two factions owing to a peculiar law regarding the care of the poor. "It seems that at that time each township was obliged to support its own paupers, the custom being to auction them off for support to the lowest bidder."[124]

Since the majority of the poor lived along the river bottoms, the responsibility for their maintenance fell primarily on the settlers on the west side of the river who could barely provide for themselves. Therefore, they petitioned to be reunited with Tuscarawas Township. But after two or three years of separation from Caldersburg, the residents decided to rejoin Jackson Township. "[Caldersburg] was rising in power and beginning to regard itself a rival of Coshocton rather than a mere appendage, and was anxious to become an independent local center." The separatists decided that they wanted to be in on the action rather than continue in their rural isolation. And so harmony was restored.

Goods sold in Caldersburg were transported by teamsters from Pittsburgh. Upon their return trip, they conveyed large quantities of venison to sell back east. "Deer were then quite numerous in the forests," historian N.N. Hill noted, "and the farmer, in wending his way to town through the bridle path, was reasonably sure of shooting a deer upon the way."[125] Some he would take home, but the remaining "saddle" of venison was sold in town for fifty cents.

Prior to the arrival of the first canalboat, the *Monticello*, on August 21, 1830, Caldersburg was a place of little consequence. There were two taverns, a dry goods store and a few shops. Coshocton fully expected that it would be the beneficiary of the canal. However, in laying out the canal, the engineers decided to run it along the west shore of the Muskingum River as a cost-cutting measure. Coshocton's loss was Caldersburg's gain. Very quickly, businesses began to pop up as close to the canal as possible in order to welcome canal travelers.

One of the canal engineers, Leander Ransom, recognized the advantages that Caldersburg had to offer, so in cooperation with Noah H. Swayne, a local lawyer, they purchased a tract of land north of the village in 1831 and platted an addition. They changed the name to Roscoe in honor of William Roscoe, an English author and abolitionist who had just passed away.

"Much of the enormous wheat crop from the cleared forest land that was shipped by canal was loaded at Roscoe, and the town bounded to the front, one of the leading shipping points along the whole canal from Portsmouth to Cleveland," historian William Bahmer recounted.[126] The center of activity was James LeRetilley's warehouse. In fact, within a very few years, Roscoe became the fourth-largest port for wheat on the 350-

mile canal system, which extended from the Great Lakes to the Hudson River. It was the epitome of a boomtown.

William Renfrew and Robert Hay initiated a distillery in 1831–32 that was later operated by the firm of Love & Hay. "In 1836 a large flouring mill was built by Arnold Medberry, Leander Ransom and John Smeltzer," but it subsequently burned some two decades later.[127] A second mill was built in 1840 by the Union Mill Company, only to be purchased by Medberry. It also burned in 1853 and subsequently moved to Coshocton.

By 1840, the population of Roscoe was 468 and Coshocton 625. "During that year, as perhaps a little later, there were in Roscoe five dry goods stores, two groceries, two forwarding houses, one fulling, two saw, and two flouring mills; while Coshocton at the same time contained six mercantile stores, one woolen factory and one flouring mill."[128] Roscoe also had a boatyard, operated by J. Balisdall, a ship carpenter, who manufactured a substantial number of canalboats. However, the *Renfrew*, one of the earliest canalboats, was built in Roscoe by Thomas B. Lewis.

When the Walhonding Canal was constructed in 1836–42, it connected with Ohio & Erie Canal at Roscoe. As a result, significant additions were made to the town in 1831, 1844 and 1849. As a boy of sixteen, James A. Garfield—future president of the United States—got his humble start driving the towpath mule that hauled a boat up and down the canal through Roscoe. With the opening of the canal and the water power of its rivers, "an impulse was given to commerce, merchandizing and manufacturing which placed the village as a business center in the front rank in Coshocton County."[129]

In June 1846, one month following President James K. Polk's declaration of war on Mexico, volunteer soldiers from Coshocton County crowded onto canalboats to begin their long trip south. Texas wanted to join the United States, but Mexico considered the annexation of the territory to be an act of war. "There was a throng to see them off, such a throng as had never assembled here before," noted historian William Bahmer, "people from the homes that the boys were leaving: women and girls forcing a cheerful goodbye through tears."[130]

As early as the 1820s, fugitives from slavery were purportedly passing through Coshocton and likely Roscoe as well. The most prominent Underground Railroad conductor in the area was a Black man, Prior Foster, who lodged runaway slaves in his shanty at Harbaugh Corner in Coshocton. However, there were more than a dozen others helping in the effort, despite the town's Democratic politics. In fact, four Underground Railroad lines converged in Roscoe Village at the Muskingum River.

A pioneering Cleveland merchant, Charles M. Giddings, was so impressed with the level of enterprise in Roscoe that he predicted that it would have a population of ten or fifteen thousand within a very few years. However, in this instance, he was wrong. "A revolution in the transportation of freight was inaugurated just as the village was blooming into a rich promise under the old regime"—the railroad![131]

The arrival of the railroad in Coshocton County changed everything. Roscoe was not located on the railroad, and by the 1860s, the town's fortunes had started to decline as the railroads began to carry most of the freight. While the canal system would continue in a fashion into the twentieth century, the Great Flood of 1913 virtually destroyed those parts that hadn't already been abandoned.

In 1881, historian N.N. Hill noted that Roscoe seemed "to have been a special object for the fury of the fire fiend, for nearly every building of any note that has had an existence here, has long been reduced to ashes."[132] These included a few flouring mills, two carding mills, a distillery, a church, two hotels, a school, a dry goods store and many other buildings of lesser consequence. And before its restoration, it was regarded as pretty much a slum.

That Roscoe has survived at all is due largely to the foresight of retired industrialist Edward E. Montgomery, who, encouraged by his wife, Frances, set out to create what he called "a living museum, so that people of the 20th century and beyond could enjoy a 'step back in time' to the 19th century where aged brick buildings, costumed interpreters and quaint shops bring the canal era back to life."[133]

Ed was the owner of the Edmont Manufacturing Company. Founded in the 1930s, the plant was the maker of the first latex-coated cotton gloves. As Ed drove through Roscoe Village on his way to work to work each day, he became increasingly discouraged by how "the once-proud canal town" had so badly deteriorated.[134] So he and his wife decided to take it upon themselves to do something about it, beginning with the restoration of the Toll House in 1968.

Built in 1840, the Toll House (406 North Whitewoman Street) was the home of Jacob Welsh, who had been a toll collector during 1836–37. Others would follow, and a decade later, the Montgomerys' restoration efforts began to pay off. From October 1978 to February 1979, NBC television broadcast a twelve-episode, twenty-five-hour-long miniseries called *Centennial*. One of the most ambitious TV shows of the period, it was based on a best-selling novel of the same name by James A. Michener, and part of it was shot in Roscoe Village. Universal Studios transformed Roscoe Village's Whitewoman Street into Lancaster, Pennsylvania, 1844, by trucking in tons of dirt to cover the paved street, camouflaging telephone poles and brick sidewalks with packing crates and barrels and hanging period signage.

Whitewoman Street, the main corridor through Roscoe Village, was named after Mary Harris, the first known person of European descent to live in Coshocton. She arrived in the area in about 1745 with a group of Mohawk Indians who had taken her captive in Deerfield, Massachusetts, in 1704 at the age of ten. She married into the Mohawk Nation and remained with them the rest of her life.

Some of the actors who came to Roscoe to film the miniseries were Greg Harrison, best known for *Trapper John, MD*, and Stephanie Zimbalist, star of *Remington Steele* opposite Pierce Brosnan.

Today, visitors to Roscoe Village can view a number of properties that date back to the canal era, as well as more recent reconstructions, and can even take a leisurely 1.5-mile ride on a horse-drawn canalboat—the *Monticello III*—on a restored section of the Ohio & Erie Canal.

Among the most notable buildings are the George LeRetilley House (427 North Whitewoman Street), built by James Retilley's son in 1853. It remains a private residence. The James LeRetilley Building (355 North Whitewoman Street) is so called because LeRetilley bought it in 1849, two years after it was

Tim and Diesel are two of the draft horses that tow the *Monticello III*. *Authors' photo.*

constructed. He arrived in Caldersburg in 1825 and opened a general store. One year later, he became the town's first postmaster.

With the arrival of the canal, LeRetilley and a business partner built a warehouse and began shipping grain. Later, he was part owner of the Union Mill Company. Until 1961, this building housed Roscoe's last post office. It is now occupied by River Ridge Leather.

Across the street is the "Mill Store" (400 North Whitewoman Street). Once used for the storage of grain, hides, wool and produce, it is an imposing, two-and-a-half-story brick and stone edifice that was erected in 1831 on the banks of the canal. Canalboats used to unload their cargo at the rear of the building, and a dry goods store once occupied the upper level. Restored in 1969, it now occupied by the Warehouse Restaurant.

Built in 1840, the William Roscoe Building (365 North Whitewoman Street) sits on the corner of Whitewoman and Mill Streets. It has served as a grocery, mortuary, restaurant and, eventually, Huck's Tavern. Restored in 1969, it also offers private apartments on the upper floors.

From 1833 to 1841, the property now known as Dr. Maro Johnson's Office (300 North Whitewoman Street) was owned by Joseph Kerr Johnson. In 1842, Dr. Johnson (no relation to Joseph) and John Burns purchased it. Six years later, Johnson bought Burns's share of the house.

However, that's just the beginning. There are numerous other things to see in Roscoe Village, including the impressive Johnson-Humrickhouse Museum.

Chapter 10

ZOAR, 1817

Tuscarawas County

"The German Quakers"

In the Kingdom of Württemberg, there was a mystical band of Christians who rejected the state church because they felt it was too secular. Following the Protestant Reformation of the 1500s, the majority of the population in what would eventually become Germany were Lutheran, while only a third were Roman Catholic. However, when the Lutheran Church adopted a new hymnal in 1791 and a new liturgy in 1808, a portion of its members broke away. They would be called Separatists.

Like other Separatist groups, the Württemberg Separatists refused to send their children to the church-controlled schools, nor would they permit their young men to serve in the military. "They abhorred all ceremonies, including marriage, confirmation, and baptism, and would not take oaths. In many respects, they resembled the Quakers, and were sometimes called the German Quakers after they arrived in the United States."[135] Their leader was Barbara Grubermann, who had been compelled to flee from her home in Switzerland because of her beliefs.

Finding refuge in southern Germany, Grubermann joined the Lutheran apostates of Württemberg, who quickly fell under her spell, likely because of her purported ability to communicate with the spirit world. "During her transports, she claimed to have journeyed to the abysses of Hell, to have talked with angels and the tortured souls of the damned, and to have seen the Devil himself."[136]

Many of the original Zoarite buildings are now private residences. *Authors' photo.*

In one of Grubermann's most celebrated visions, she claimed she was given an audience with God and Jesus Christ and that God had bestowed on her and her followers a title: "We, by the grace of God, children of the Most High, enlightened by the Holy Writ, admirers of Jehovah and of the everlasting majesty of God, warriors under the flag of Jesus, who is and remains the Prince of our souls, Wonderful, Councilor, Power, Grace, Holy Father, and Prince of Peace!"[137]

Mother Ann Lee of the Shakers and Barbara Heinemann of the Amana Society experienced similar trances in which they purportedly received divine revelations. Grubermann insisted that her followers must immediately separate themselves from the evil of the world because the long-hoped-for millennium—Christ's Second Coming—was at hand.[138] As Joseph Baumeler (also known as Joseph Bäumler or Bimeler) recalled, "We were clearly given to know that God judges the world and will punish her for her sins but that He will preserve those who turn to Him....Led by these insights we saw it necessary to separate ourselves from the godless, worldly life and all sinful customs and habits."[139] With reluctance, he took Grubermann's place when she died and led them to America.

Because Grubermann had told them that they had to act quickly and could not afford to deliberate, the Separatists were not particularly well prepared for what awaited them in New World. Upon their arrival in Philadelphia in 1817, they purchased some land sight-unseen in Tuscarawas County, Ohio. Although the original plan had been for each Separatist to pay for his own share of the land from whatever profit he realized from the sale of his harvest, many had been too needy to work their own land and had to take jobs with their neighbors just to survive. In addition, they were too few able-bodied men and women and too many children and elderly.

By December 1, 1817, Baumeler and an advanced party had built the first log hut on site of what would become the village of Zoar. They were joined the next spring by the remainder of their group and set about planting a few crops. However, the following winter was so severe that nearly all of the Zoarites' crops failed. It was only through the generosity of their neighbors that they were able to avoid starvation. With so much of their land undeveloped and many of their band compelled to look for work elsewhere, it became evident that they were in danger of defaulting on their mortgage.

As historian Charles Nordhoff later wrote:

> *Early in 1819 the leaders after consultation determined that, to succeed, they must draw in to themselves all whom poverty had compelled to take service at a distance. This resolution was laid before the whole society, and, after some weeks of discussion, was agreed to; and on the 15th of April articles of agreement for a community of goods were signed. There were then about two hundred and twenty-five persons—men, women, and children.*[140]

Despite Baumeler's vocal opposition—he feared that the plan simply wouldn't work—the Zoarites formed what they called "eine gute Gemeinschaft" (a good community). But Baumeler, for once, was wrong. "Almost from the first day of their existence as a communal society, the fortunes of the Zoarites underwent a complete reversal. They became prosperous. They could afford to be charitable to their neighbors in the Tuscarawas valley. They were free."[141] According to Morhart's *The Zoar Story*:

> *The Zoarites selected their own metaphor in the magnificent garden which was the focal point of the community. Designed by Joseph Baumeler, the leader of the community, in the shape of a wheel, it represented the New Jerusalem mentioned in the Book of Revelation. A tall Norway spruce in*

> *the center stood for Christ and life everlasting. It was encircled by a hedge of arbor vitae, around which ran a green path which symbolized the Kingdom of God. Twelve Irish juniper trees, one for each apostle, stood just outside the path, and twelve paths radiated out from the center path to the edges of the garden like spokes. These represented the many different walks of life leading to Heaven.*[142]

Once in the New World, the Zoarites became an even more unconventional group by preserving their Old World customs—much like the Quakers and the Amish. For example, they continued to speak among themselves in the Swabian dialect of their native Württemberg, but most learned English as well. They also maintained the same manner of dress that was characteristic of the Old World. And just like the Quakers, they addressed both friends and strangers as "thee" and "thou" ("dich" and "du" in German). Many of them went so far as to fashion a many-pointed star out of cardboard decorated with thread and wore it to signify their membership in the group. Such symbolic practices helped to remind them that they were to keep their distance from those who were more worldly.

Owing to the need for women to work and not be burden by caring for children, the Zoarities also instituted celibacy in 1822 in the name of keeping their group together. However, just three years later, the Zoarites signed a contract to hand-dig the seven miles of the Ohio & Erie Canal that would bisect their property. With the $21,000 they earned, they were able to pay off their mortgage and end their vow of celibacy in 1829. The canal also provided the Separatists with a mean of shipping their produce and other goods to Cleveland. And so they thrived.

When cholera swept through the colony in 1834, carried by canalboat passengers, the Zoarites did not lose hope. Although fifty of them died, Baumeler, their concerned leader, moved freely among them. "He seemed to have a charmed life, for neither disease nor accident had power to quench his dauntless spirit."[143] During his visit to Zoar, historian William Hinds suggested to one Zoarite, "Joseph Baumeler was a remarkable man, I judge." "Yes," the Zoarite replied, "when he was our leader we knew everything would come out right."[144]

However, not every member of the community shared that assessment. As early as 1849, there was a faction that agitated for the division of their assets. They pointed out that Baumeler rode in a carriage while everyone else walked. But then, he also had a limp. Furthermore, he lived in an impressive brick home with a balcony, piazzas and a cupola, while they lived in more modest dwellings. However, they were ignoring the fact that the home was originally built to house the elderly, and the Separatists felt that their leader should inhabit it.

Although Baumeler managed Zoar during its peak years, membership was already declining. After celibacy was discontinued, he was among the first to take a wife, but the birthrate in the community did not compensate for the death rate. Then, in 1853, Baumeler passed away, and everything changed. There was no single Zoarite who could replace him. The role of agent general, which had been created for Baumeler, was quickly abolished.

By design, Baumeler had been both their temporal and spiritual leader. The Zoarites did not want to establish a separate priesthood. However, there was no one in the community who possessed the necessary administrative talent and religious wisdom. Much like the Quakers, Baumeler believed that everyone had their own inner light, which led them to worship as they saw fit. However, his "sermons" were so highly valued that the Zoarites had transcribed and published them and continued to read them at their religious services after he had passed away.

Jacob Ackermann eventually succeeded, but never truly replaced, Baumeler. He had everyone's respect for his kindness and dedication to the community and so was chosen as their leader. However, he was accorded no more constitutional authority than his fellow trustees. The society would henceforth be run by a committee. No one man was authorized to act on behalf of the Separatist Society of Zoar. Instead, the trustees procured a seal "containing the device of a Garden surrounded by a circular wreath of flowers with the letters 'ZOAR' between the Garden and the wreath."[145] This would be the Zoarites' official emblem, and all of the trustees would affix their signatures beneath it.

Under this arrangement, the Zoarites lumbered along until 1898. Their economy declined following the Civil War, and their membership had embraced more material values. This time they did not have the strong leadership of a Baumeler to stand up against the faction that demanded a division of assets. When the proposition was put to a vote, the majority agreed, and the Separatist Society of Zoar was dissolved, after just short of eighty years.

Near the end of the community's existence, Karl Knortz, a visitor to Zoar, asked the meaning of the garden; he discovered that few of the Zoarites could tell him. Dr. Breiter finally explained to him that "our young people are too worldly to take any interest in such things.…[Y]ou will have noticed a broad path which winds around the whole garden; this is the path which is tread by the people of worldly inclinations, wherefore they always arrive at the sinful goal from which they originally started, but never arrive at the heavenly Jerusalem."[146]

More than a century later, visitors to Zoar are treated to a unique historical site in that some of the properties are owned and managed by the Ohio History Connection, while others remain in private hands. Most of the community was listed in the National Register of Historic Places in 1969. Among the highlights are the following.

Number One House, built in 1835, is located at the southwest corner of Main and 3rd Streets. Standing two and a half stories tall, the brick and sandstone structure became the home of Joseph Baumeler. Owned by the Ohio History Connection, it has been operated as a museum since 1935. Directly behind Number One House and attached by a breezeway are the Dining Room, Kitchen, Laundry and Magazine.

The Bakery, located on the northwest corner of Main and 4th Streets, was built between 1880 and 1882 in response to the influx of railroad workers to the village. Although somewhat smaller than the main bakery, it was a hive of activity, especially when the children stopped by after school to pick up bread for their families.

The second Sewing House, Number Five, was built in the 1840s. In addition to three rooms that were reserved for sewing, it also served as the home of Jacob Kuemerle and his family. Owned by the Ohio History Connection, it is currently being used by an artisan co-op.

Built in 1835, the Garden House Number Eleven was the home of Simon Beuter and his family. As the village gardener, Simon tended the one-acre ornamental garden in the center of Zoar with the assistance of a crew composed of young teenage boys. Later, a greenhouse was added to Simon's two-story brick home.

Number Twenty-Seven House—the Bimeler House & Museum—was built in 1863 and occupied by William and Lillian Ruof Bimeler. Located on the southeast corner of Park and 3rd Streets, it is a two-and-a-half-story brick structure that has been extensively restored. Lillian later donated it to the Ohio History Connection.

The Zoar Store, built in 1833, was the headquarters of the Separatist Society of Zoar, as well as a general store and a post office. Located on the southwest corner of Main and 2nd Streets, it is where the Zoarites, who did not use cash, made their purchases. Today, it serves as an information center and gift shop.

Immediately behind the Zoar store is the Dairy/Springhouse, which was built in 1841. Butter and cheese were made there for the members of the society as well as the public.

The Town Hall, located on the west side of Main between 3rd and 2nd Streets, was one of the last buildings constructed by the Zoarites. Built in 1887, it housed everything from the barbershop to the fire department and even the jail. It was also where the Zoar band gave concerts from the second-floor porch roof, and dances were held there on Saturday nights. The village government is now housed here, along with two museums.

The Zoar Hotel is situated at the southeast corner of Main and 2nd Streets. Built in 1833, it had forty sleeping rooms, a large dining room and a clientele that included everyone from beggars to President William McKinley. Although a wing that contained fifty more sleeping rooms was added in 1892, it was razed in the late 1940s. The structure is currently undergoing renovation.

The remainder of Zoar is privately owned, but most of the buildings have identifying markers that explain their significance. Visitors can avail themselves of a guided tour or stroll about the village on their own and imagine what life was like in the nineteenth century.

Chapter 11

KIRTLAND, 1831

Lake County

"The First Mormon Temple"

Under a royal charter issued in 1662, the borders of the colony of Connecticut extended "from sea-to-sea."[147] But other royal grants had created the colonies of New York and Pennsylvania, which encroached on Connecticut's claim. This conflict was eliminated with the ratification of the U.S. Constitution, which required states with "trans-Appalachian land claims" to surrender them to the newly formed government.[148] Nevertheless, Connecticut was permitted to keep a 120-mile strip of land as compensation. The northern boundary was set at 42 degrees, 2 minutes north latitude (basically, the middle of Lake Erie) and the southern at 41 degrees (just below Youngstown). This area was designated New Connecticut or Connecticut Western Reserve.

When the Treaty of Greenville was signed in 1795, nearly three-quarters of the Western Reserve became available for settlement, safe from depredation by Indians. The State of Connecticut promptly sold this land to the Connecticut Land Company for $1.2 million. However, it was slow to attract settlers because the land was mostly unsuitable for farming. It wasn't until 1810–12 that the first European American families began arriving in Kirtland. The village of Kirtland was named for Turhand Kirtland, a stockholder in the land company and a judge in Trumbull County who was known for his fairness in dealing with the local Native Americans. In 1818, Kirtland Township was organized. The following year, Old South Congregational Church was organized and a frame schoolhouse built.

The John Johnson Inn was reconstructed on its original site. *Authors' photo.*

Meanwhile, 250 miles away, Joseph Smith Jr. received his "First Vision" in Palmyra, New York, during the spring of 1820. One of eleven children, Smith was a fourteen-year-old farm boy whose family had endured a series of crop failures, causing them to relocate from his birthplace in Sharon, Vermont. At the time, the Palmyra region was a "hotbed of religious enthusiasm during the Second Great Awakening."[149] The entire Smith family became caught up in the excitement. Both his parents and a grandfather claimed that they had experienced dreams or visions in which they communicated with God. Joseph said that he had seen "two personages" whom he later indicated were God and Jesus Christ.

Three years later, Joseph said that an angel came to him and showed him how to find the spot where a book of golden plates was buried. On them were inscribed a Judeo-Christian history of an ancient American civilization that he identified as a lost tribe of Israel. And Joseph would also proclaim that the American Indians were descended from this tribe. In 1830, he published his translation of these plates called the Book of Mormon and also organized the Church of Christ. He then began to preach that his purpose was to restore the early Christian Church.

In an incredibly short period of time, Joseph was able to attract a committed band of followers. Among them was Oliver Cowdery, who immediately set out west to proselytize the "Laminites" (i.e., American Indians). He impressed them with the fact they were included in the Book of Mormon. Along the way, he and his men established a branch of the new church in Kirtland, which then numbered just over one thousand people. Among those who joined were Sidney Rigdon, a Baptist minister, and Newel K. Whitney, owner of the general store. By the end of the year, all Latter-day Saints, as Joseph called them, were urged to relocate to Ohio. This would be the church's headquarters for the next eight years.

With the completion of the Erie Canal in northern New York, those who wished to move westward could travel to Ohio via Lake Erie. In 1831, Joseph Smith was commanded by God to go to Ohio, where he and the Saints would receive "His law, be endowed with power from on high, and prepare to share His gospel among all nations."[150] Along with his followers, he set out to build a communal American Zion. Their first stop was Kirtland, but they also established an outpost in Independence, Missouri. Independence was intended to be the center of the Mormon Church.

No doubt due to Joseph's presence, Kirtland quickly became the fastest-growing Mormon community.[151] Joseph also began experiencing many visions. At a general conference of the church held in Kirtland, the first high priests were ordained. Many of the most prominent leaders were converts from Sidney Rigdon's church. And some of the Elders were dispatched to Jackson County, Missouri, to form yet another settlement. Not long afterward, Joseph received a revelation that Jackson County was the site of Zion. Meanwhile, he and his wife, Emma, moved in with the John and Elsa Johnson family (6203 Pioneer Trail) in Hiram, Ohio, thirty miles south. While many of his followers continued to come to Kirtland, others migrated to Missouri.

One year after his arrival in Ohio, Joseph was seized by a mob at the Johnson house, beaten and then tarred and feathered along with Sidney Rigdon. Both men were left for dead. (The Johnson home has since been carefully restored to its condition when Joseph and Emma lived there.) The following day, after Emma had nursed his wounds and cleansed the tar and feathers from his skin, Joseph gave a sermon. And he had yet another revelation at the end of this year—this one was to build a temple in Kirtland. Meanwhile, following a period of mental imbalance, Rigdon displaced Cowdery as a leader in the church and even went so far as to challenge Joseph's leadership on one occasion. He was especially vocal about building a temple.

Early in 1833, Joseph started the School of Prophets in Whitney's store. In another revelation, Joseph shared the "Word of Wisdom," the Latter-day Saints' code of health, which discourages smoking and drinking, while encouraging consumption of proper foods. Two years after Smith's arrival in Kirtland, the number of Mormons living there had increased to 150.

In 1836, the Kirtland Temple was dedicated by Joseph with some nine hundred to one thousand people in attendance. It was an impressive structure given the times and the resources available. By then, there were some two thousand Latter-day Saints living in the area. On Easter Sunday, he and Cowdery both experienced visions of heavenly messengers while in the temple, including Jesus, Moses, Elias and Elijah. Other church leaders also saw many spiritual manifestations.

In January 1837, Joseph made a major misstep when he established the Kirtland Safety Society, aka Kirtland Safety Society Anti-Banking Company. It was a joint stock company intended to serve the needs of the Mormons, but Joseph had failed to obtain a state charter. It was forced to close in November due to a combination of poor management and the nationwide economic Panic of 1837. Many blamed Joseph for the bank's failure and believed that it was a scheme to enrich himself.

Among Joseph's former supporters who turned on him was Oliver Cowdery. He accused Joseph of having had a sexual relationship with Fanny Alger, a teenage servant employed in his home. It has been alleged that she was the first of some forty plural wives the church founder would take. Meanwhile, Cowdery was excommunicated for his accusation against Joseph.

In January of the following year, Joseph and his family left Kirtland for Missouri due to continuing financial problems and the religious persecution that had grown since the bank closure. One year earlier, an outsider observed, "There is as many Mormons going away as there is coming in this Summer....[T]hey are at war among themselves."[152] Six months later, an Urbana, Ohio newspaper reported:

> *On Thursday last about sixty wagons, accompanied by upwards of five hundred Mormons, passed through this place on their way to the "Promised Land," in Missouri. They are from Kirtland...and have with them their cattle, furniture, &c.... These followers of Rigdon and Smith will probably not find quite as much "milk and honey" in Missouri as then anticipate.*[153]

Along with officially moving the headquarters of the church to Missouri, Joseph renamed it the Church of Jesus Christ of Latter-day Saints.

During the 1840s and 1850s, Kirtland Temple was leased as a schoolhouse by the Western Reserve Teachers Seminary. Rumor has it the building also served as a stable. However, Joseph Smith was not finished with Kirtland yet. In 1841, he received another revelation that proclaimed, "I, the Lord, will build up Kirtland."[154] This revelation became known as the Kirtland Prophecy. However, it did not prove to be. In June 1844, Joseph and his brother, Hyrum, were murdered by a mob in the Carthage Jail, Hancock County, Illinois. He left no designated successor. Two years later, the reins of the main body of the church would be taken up by Brigham Young.

After Joseph and his followers decamped for the west, ownership of the Kirtland Temple was unclear. A group called the Reorganized Church of Jesus Christ of the Latter-day Saints, an offshoot of the original church through Joseph's son Joseph Smith III, took the matter to court. They eventually obtained title on the principle of adverse possession (i.e., "squatter's rights"). Now called the Community of Christ, they provide tours of the temple.

Joseph Smith III sought to wrest control of the Mormon Church in Utah and rejected the authority of Brigham Young and subsequent claimants to the prophet's mantle. He was particularly opposed to the practice of plural marriage. However, once the Latter-day Saints in Utah rejected polygamy as well, the line separating the two factions more or less disappeared. Over time, the Reorganized Church failed to grow at the same rate.

Mark Staker, a Mormon historian, summed up Joseph Smith's Ohio legacy in this way: "Although clearly the most significant part of the Kirtland experience in the lives of Latter-day Saints included the revelations that came to their prophet while living there, many of which were published in the Doctrine and Covenants, even the history, context, and meaning of these significant documents became increasingly obscure over time."[155] Brigham Young predicted that other revelations would possibly prove to be mysterious to their own children—those who did not have personal knowledge of the circumstances under which they were delivered.

Up to twenty or thirty of the old high priests in Kirtland had rebelled against Joseph Smith's leadership and founded a new church. In response, Joseph asked those who were loyal to him to gather up their families and move west as quickly as possible. In fact, Joseph Smith and Sidney Rigdon left at once. The Kirtland Saints who followed them believed that Missouri would turn out to be the promised land—that it would be the New Jerusalem. In a subsequent revelation, Joseph said that the Kirtland properties should be sold to pay off the failed bank's remaining debts.

However, some of those who remained behind still felt some loyalty to Joseph and hoped to maintain Kirtland as a spiritual center. In 1840, Joseph named one of them, Almon Babbitt, to the office of stake president of Kirtland and announced in a letter, "It has been deemed prudent to advise the eastern brethren who desire to locate in Kirtland, to do so."[156] Three months later, however, Joseph grew so alarmed about how zealously Babbitt was carrying out his instructions that he accused him in another revelation of setting up a "golden calf for the worship of me people."[157]

The church of the Latter-day Saints was born in New York and spent its early childhood in Ohio. After a difficult adolescence in Missouri and Illinois, it settled in Utah. Here it reached maturity. In the course of two hundred years, it has grown to nearly 17 million members worldwide through its strong sense of community, family orientation and proselytizing missionary outreach. Although many Mormons self-identify as Christians, many Christians disagree because of the Saints' belief that Joseph Smith was chosen to restore Christ's church and that living apostles and prophets continue to guide them.

In addition to the Kirtland Temple (9020 Chillicothe Road), visitors to Kirtland can tour the Kirtland Historic North Cemetery (aka Kirtland Temple Cemetery), where some of the early Saints were buried, including Joseph Smith's grandmother and Oliver Cowdery's parents. There are also a number of buildings—both original and reproductions—that are relevant to the church's history.

Joseph and Emma Smith acquired a home in Kirtland (8989 Chillicothe Road) late in 1833 across the street from where Joseph opened a store. He would continue to live in it until he left Ohio in 1838. Both structures have been renovated and are open to the public

Historic Kirtland (7800 Kirtland-Chardon Road) contains a visitor's center and six historic structures. There is a replica of the Kirtland Flats Schoolhouse, which was built in 1819 prior to the arrival the Latter-day Saint missionaries. It played an important role in the community, both for public education and community gatherings. However, the original burned down in the 1860s. There are also reproductions of the ashery and sawmill utilized by the Mormons, constructed to illustrate the types of industry they operated in Kirtland. Other buildings in Historic Kirtland include the Newel K. Whitney Store, the Whitney Home and the Johnson Inn.

Newel K. Whitney, an early Mormon convert, built a general store in 1826. It also served as a post office, bishop's storehouse and early church headquarters. It was here where Joseph purportedly was commanded by God to build the Kirtland Temple. The building has been completely restored.

Sidney Rigdon, one of Joseph Smith's earliest converts, lived in this house with his wife, Phoebe. *Authors' photo.*

By 1827, Peter French had converted his two-story brick home into a tavern. Six years later, the Latter-day Saints purchased the tavern and assigned John Johnson to manage it. The same year, Joseph Smith introduced the office of the patriarch while at the tavern and ordained his father as patriarch to the church. In addition to providing rooms and meals for travelers, the tavern served as an office building meeting room, print shop and social hall. The tavern burned down in 1815 but was rebuilt in 2002.

About 1824, following the birth of their first child, Newel and Elizabeth Ann Whitney built a two-story, wood-frame home. They were among the early converts to the Mormon Church and had welcomed Joseph and Emma Smith into their home in 1831. While living with the Whitneys, Joseph received several revelations and established the office of bishop, which Newel was later called to serve.

Say what you will about Joseph Smith, but he was never boring.

Chapter 12

OBERLIN, 1833

Lorain County

"The Town that Started the Civil War"

As Kornblith and Lasser wrote in *Elusive Utopia*, "Oberlin's story begins with John Jay Shipherd, a religious visionary and Oberlin's founding father. Born in 1802 into a well-to-do, politically prominent, white, slaveholding family in upstate New York, Shipherd from his youth desired to preach the gospel."[158] After taking his first ministerial position in Vermont in 1827, he decided three years later that God wanted him to go westward. Arriving by steamboat in Cleveland late in 1830, he was quickly hired as minister of the First Presbyterian Church in Elyria.

However, Shipherd did not consider himself to be a talented preacher. And after he called on his congregation to forsake alcohol, he was removed from his post. At this point, Shipherd began thinking about founding "a small, intentional community dedicated to the glorification of God and the Christian conversion of mankind."[159] To assist him in carrying out his plan, he called on his childhood friend and a former missionary to the Choctaw Indians in Mississippi, Philo Penfield Stewart.

At the time, Stewart and his wife were living with Shipherd, his wife and their children. He had moved to Elyria to prepare for his own ordination by his old friend. As their model, they looked to Pastor John Frederic Oberlin's ministry among the Ban de la Roche, a small group of people in Alsace, France. In fact, they would name their own colony Oberlin in his honor.

Choosing a heavily forested site nine miles southwest of Elyria, they arranged to purchase the land—some seven thousand acres—while soliciting

The home of Wilson Bruce Evans, a freeborn Black man who took part in the Oberlin-Wellington Rescue. *Authors' photo.*

donations and recruiting settlers back east. A key factor in closing the deal was the agreement by the owners, a couple of Connecticut merchants, to donate five hundred acres for an educational institution.

All would-be settlers were required to sign the Covenant of Oberlin Colony, a document that set forth the purpose of the colony as well as the obligations of membership. What it offered to those who joined was "a profoundly communitarian and ascetic way of life."[160] They were to glorify God and strive to do good, while exercising self-discipline and self-denial. It was very much a religious order that they were joining.

Surprisingly, perhaps, Shipherd found some takers. By the time he and his family had moved to Oberlin in 1833, the community had a population of fifty or so—a dozen families and a few single people. Three months later, Oberlin Collegiate Institute opened with thirty-four students, with another forty expected soon. Its motto was and still is "Learning and Labor." In March 1834, a circular stated that the school's goal was "to give the most useful education at the least expense of health, time, and money; and to extend the benefits of such education to both sexes; and all classes of community as far as it means will allow."[161] When four women enrolled in 1837, Oberlin became the first coeducational college in the nation.

Although the institute's surprisingly progressive purpose and the colony's strikingly conservative one seemed at odds, Shipherd had no difficulty reconciling them. Both were ultimately intended to hasten the arrival of God's kingdom on Earth. They were creating a Christian religious community to train Christian missionaries to Christianize the American frontier.

The plan for the colony was a reflection of its communitarian foundation. It was a 5,500-acre square, roughly three miles on each side. One road ran east–west, the other north–south, crossing at the very center of the village. "Immediately to the southwest of the intersection was the public square, which in turn was bordered on the south by the Institute's combined boardinghouse and classroom building. Surrounding this compact town core were square and rectangular lots ranging in size from 40 to 169 acres."[162]

Unlike a true communal society, Oberlin's thirty-five families owned their own land. Most of them had both a small central lot where they maintained their residence and a larger peripheral one that they farmed, much the same as Worthington had. However, they were discouraged from owning more property than they had need of, nor were they supposed to accumulate excess wealth. But of course, some did.

Also in 1834, the community organized the Congregational Church of Christ at Oberlin.[163] In 1842, an impressive edifice was built that still stands and is known familiarly as First Church. Led by abolitionist Charles Grandison Finney, it has hosted Frederick Douglass, Ralph Waldo Emerson, Booker T. Washington, Mark Twain and Dr. Martin Luther King. By 1860, it had the largest congregation in the country, necessitating the construction of Second Church.

When Oberlin was founded, it was not an abolitionist community per se. However, that would change with the enrollment of the "Lane Rebels" in 1835. A group of several dozen young men under the leadership of abolitionist Theodore Weld, they had withdrawn from Lane Theological Seminary in Cincinnati owing to its treatment of the Black community and reluctance to speak out against slavery.

The Rebels had crossed paths with Shipherd while he was out recruiting students, and they agreed to enroll at Oberlin Institute on two conditions. The first was that the school pledged not to interfere with free speech. The second was that the school accept students irrespective of color—something no college in the United States was yet doing. Shipherd agreed, and the trustees reluctantly supported him, although the first two Black students did not enroll in Oberlin proper, but rather at Sheffield Manual Labor Institute, an affiliated school.[164] This was a big change for Shipherd, who had been brought up to accept slavery and only later had had come to recognize "his sinful prejudice."[165]

Although Philo Stewart and his wife had pledged to serve the institute for five years, he was at odds with his colleagues when it came to their extreme abolitionist ideas and also the issue of admitting Black students. Stewart feared that admitting students of color would threaten the coeducational school's program, and in fact, critics raised the issue of miscegenation as an argument against doing so. Therefore, despite having been an abolitionist all his life, he resigned in 1836 and returned east, but not before he had patented the Oberlin stove—an early compact, cast-iron, wood-burning cookstove—and assigned the rights to the Oberlin Collegiate Institute for five years.

Not satisfied with founding one college, in 1836 Shipherd tried to establish another in Lansing, Michigan. Called Grand River Seminary, it failed. One year later, he announced that he was going to open another school in Lagrange County, Indiana, but it never developed. Finally, in 1843, he went to Eaton County, Michigan, intent on finding a spot for another colony and school. It was to be Olivet College. However, in the process, he contracted malaria and died before the school opened at the end of the year.

During this period, the original Covenant of Oberlin Colony seemed to be falling by the wayside as other progressive ideas competed for attention. "Perfectionist radicalism and attendant causes, including the Graham vegetarian diet, female moral reform, temperance, missionary activity, and particularly antislavery activism, permeated early Oberlin."[166] As a consequence, many African Americans—some free people of color, others fugitives from slavery—began settling in the vicinity of Oberlin. The town soon became a station on the Underground Railroad, both because it was relatively safe there and also because of its proximity to Lake Erie and Canada just beyond.

The most famous Underground Railroad incident was the Oberlin-Wellington Rescue, in which a large group of both white and Black residents of Oberlin successfully rescued a fugitive named John Price from nearby Wellington but then were tried for their for their actions.[167] It was this incident that gave birth to Oberlin's nickname, the "Town that Started the Civil War." Both Oberlin students and faculty enlisted during the Civil War, and African American alumni of the college led the way in the recruitment of the state's first soldiers of color.

However, not all residents of Oberlin were antislavery. One of the most "violent pro-slavery" Democrats, for reasons that cannot be explained, was a Black man. Allen Jones was quite outspoken in his hatred for those of African ancestry.[168] He was joined by two white men, Lewis D. Boynton and Chauncey Wack. Boyton was the leader of the Democratic Party in Lorain County, and Wack operated Oberlin's second hotel, where he welcomed visiting slavecatchers.

Among the most prominent African Americans in Oberlin was John Mercer Langston. After graduating from the college, he became the first Black lawyer in Ohio, the first person of his race to hold elective office in the United States and the first person of color elected to Congress from Virginia. He also was active in the Underground Railroad and led the National Equal Rights League. "For many years Langston [was] the preeminent 'bridge' figure in Oberlin, moving comfortably in both black and white circles and facilitating interracial collaboration within the community."[169]

But with the end of the Civil War and the passage of the Fifteenth Amendment, Oberlin's men of color sought to take an active role in the governance of the community. This led to a division in the Republican Party owing to a difference in priorities between white Republicans and Black Republicans. Although there were African Americans holding such important positions as trustee, constable, street commissioner and deputy marshal, the Black voters did not feel there was enough progress in protecting their civil rights. The split that was developing within the Republican Party was epitomized by the election of Democrat Chauncey Wick to the town council as a Republican.

During the early 1880s, racially segregated seating became an issue in the Ladies Hall dining room at the college. It was blamed on wealthy students who brought "class prejudice" with them. Later, the blame was shifted to "poor whites." Whatever the cause, a "color line" had appeared in Oberlin as the community became increasingly segregated. As Kornblith and Lasser declared in *Elusive Utopia*, "While the college proudly enshrined its antislavery past, it failed to engage in the continuing struggle for racial equality. The priorities of the college, like those of the town, shifted with the time."[170]

According to the 1880 census, African Americans represented 21 percent of the population of Oberlin. Having failed to keep up with the white residents financially, the town's people of color were beginning to seek their fortunes elsewhere, among them some of their most prominent champions. Carol Lasser noted, "Despite a post-Reconstruction retreat from racial egalitarian principle, at Oberlin in the late nineteenth century, one-third of all African American graduates of predominantly white colleges before 1900 were Oberlin alumni."[171]

While there was much hand-wringing and occasional calls to action over the intervening century, Oberlin still struggles with its failure to live up to the standards it set for itself at the time of its founding. In their history of Oberlin, Kornblith and Lasser concluded with this assertion: "The persistent optimism in Oberlinians' intermittent rededications to the principle of racial equality is the closest thing to a happy ending that this study has to offer."[172]

In 2017, Oberlin College appointed Carmen Twillie Ambar as the school's first Black president (and second woman), 188 years after its founding.

Today, the visitor to Oberlin can still view many historic sites, although some are frustratingly missing, having been razed over the years. For example, there are numerous old homes, some dating back to before the Civil War. One of the most notable is that of John Mercer Langston, Ohio's first African American lawyer, abolitionist and Republican congressman from Virginia. Another is the home of another prominent abolitionist and philanthropist, Jabez Lyman Burrell, who also served as a trustee of the college. Then there is the Wack-Dietz House, the residence of Southern sympathizer Chauncey Wack, who testified against the Oberlin-Wellington rescuers. Just across the street from Wack's house is that of Wilson B. Evans, an African American carpenter who participated in the rescue.

The Frank Fanning Jewett House, owned by a former chemistry professor, is now part of the Oberlin Heritage Center. The former home of Oberlin's

The home of Chauncey Wack, Evans's neighbor, who was a prosecution witness against the Oberlin-Wellington rescuers. *Authors' photo.*

most prominent capitalist, the Albert H. Johnson House was converted into a college dormitory. Johnson was a banker and railroad president. The home of James and Marianne Dascomb, an Oberlin professor and the head of the women's department, respectively, is the town's finest example of the Gothic Revival style.

There are also many vintage buildings, including First Church, the early center of community life; Christ Church, the second church to be built in Oberlin; the Goodrich Block, built in 1882 after the historic downtown fire; Union School, built in 1873–74 to serve all grades; the Railroad Depot, which brought many students to Oberlin beginning in 1866; Oberlin Gas Lighting Company Gasholder Building, a rare surviving coal gas storage facility; Little Red Schoolhouse, the town's original one-room school; and the Old Water Tower, built of quarried sandstone.

Not to be overlooked are historic places such as Westwood Cemetery—which is the final resting place for college presidents, Civil War soldiers and fugitives from slavery—and Memorial Arch, commemorating the Oberlin missionaries and their children killed in the Chinese Boxer Rebellion.

In all, there are thirty-nine buildings designated as "Oberlin Historic Landmarks." Twenty of them are in the National Register of Historic Places. The Oberlin Heritage Center is exceptionally tourist friendly.

Chapter 13

HAYDENVILLE, 1852

Hocking County

"The Last Company Town"

What to do with Haydenville? Even the most ardent preservationist must admit that it would require millions of dollars to stabilize the community's various structures, let alone restore them, yet the town's commercial prospects are few. As a result, Haydenville has no champions—none with money, that is. Meanwhile, this architectural oddity is slowly crumbling to dust.

Known as Ohio's last company town, Haydenville was also one of its first. Peter Hayden (1806–88), its namesake, initially came to Columbus in 1835. Quickly recognizing that "Central Ohio abounded in timber useful for certain kinds of manufacturing [he] immediately made propositions for employment of the Penitentiary convicts, most of whom were then idle."[173] The employment of prison labor was an idea Hayden had used as far back as 1821 at New York's Auburn Prison, when he hired inmates to make woodworking planes. It made good economic sense. The prisoners worked cheaper than ordinary laborers.

Relocating to Columbus in 1845, Hayden operated a foundry and saddlery in part with the assistance of convict labor from the Ohio Penitentiary. The most impressive of the family's businesses would be the so-called Birmingham Works on the east bank of the Scioto River. The main building was a limestone edifice nearly 200 feet long and four stories tall, with two 75-foot-long wings. It produced up to eight tons of chain and

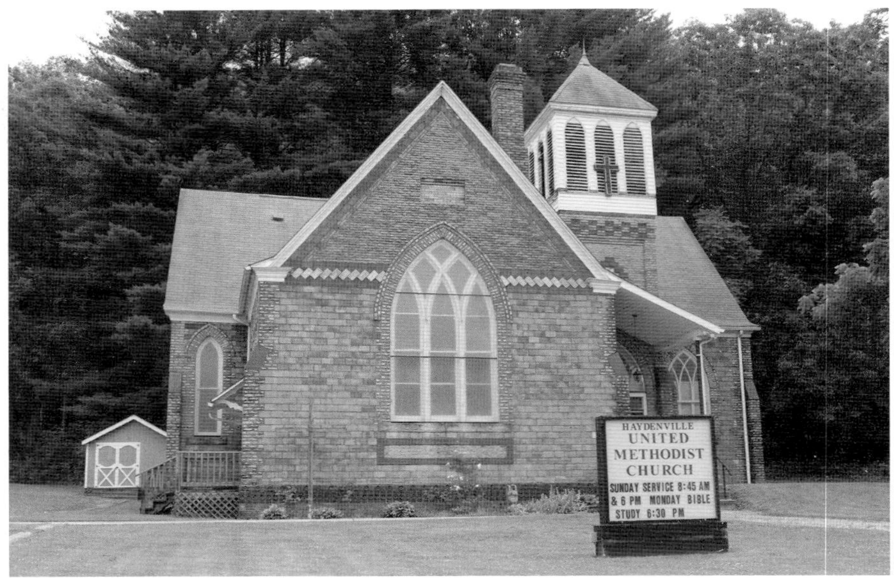

The Haydenville United Methodist Church was built with locally produced materials. *Dan Keck/Wikipedia.*

three tons of iron rods each day. There was also a smith's shop some 115 feet long by 32 wide. It produced three tons of wire. From 100 to 150 men were employed there.

Meanwhile, as historian Alfred Lee noted, Hayden's New York business interests continued to expand, "and in due course of events he started an additional factory at Newark, New Jersey, and made engagements for employment of prison labor in California. For the sale of his large product, resulting from these various enterprises, Mr. Hayden opened wholesale stores in the principal cities, east and west."[174] However, a plant in Galveston, Texas, was confiscated by the Confederacy during the early months of the Civil War.

In order to obtain the necessary raw materials and fuel for his factories, Hayden bought large tracts of coal in the Hocking Valley. By 1847, he had formed a partnership with J.F. Somers of Nelsonville under the name Hayden & Somers. They opened a store in Nelsonville that dealt in dry goods, groceries and hardware but also coal, which they shipped to Columbus via the canal system. This was his first venture into the Hocking Valley, but he immediately recognized the opportunity it represented. One year later, he began construction on a three-story house with a fourth-floor

SunWatch, a thirteenth-century Indian village, is being reconstructed in Dayton. *Ford Walker photo.*

The Moravian Indian village of Schoenbrunn was rebuilt in the early twentieth century. *Authors' photo.*

A monument at Gnadenhütten commemorates the massacre of peaceful Moravian Indians. *Authors' photo.*

The 1899 Lockmaster's House stands in Marietta beside the Muskingum River. *Authors' photo.*

Harmar Village is a historic neighborhood across the Muskingum River from Marietta. *Authors' photo.*

The oldest continually used commercial building in Ohio is in Worthington. *Authors' photo.*

The historic Worthington Inn began as a private residence in 1831. *Authors' photo.*

The Ohio Yearly Meeting House in Mount Pleasant dates back to 1814. *Authors' photo.*

In 1804, Enoch Harris opened a general store in this Mount Pleasant cabin. *Authors' photo.*

Denison University in Granville has an impressive collection of buildings. *Authors' photo.*

John Rankin and his family lived in this home some three hundred feet above Ripley. *Authors' photo.*

Lindey's, a popular German Village restaurant, was once known as the Bucket of Blood. *Authors' photo.*

This warehouse was built on the banks of the Ohio & Erie Canal in Roscoe Village. *Ford Walker photo.*

Joseph Bimeler's cabin is the oldest home still standing in Zoar. *Authors' photo.*

The combination Garden House with adjoining Greenhouse in Zoar. *Authors' photo.*

The first temple built by Joseph Smith and his followers is in Kirtland. *Authors' photo.*

The First Church in Oberlin was once the moral center of the community. *Authors' photo.*

Of the eighteen silo houses once built in the vicinity of Haydenville, only one remains. *Authors' photo.*

Haydenville was intended to be a workingman's utopia. *Authors' photo.*

An aerial view of the Fort Hayes campus, showing the mixture of old and new buildings. *Jsjessee/Wikipedia.*

The railroad depot at Dennison welcomed thousands of troops during World War II. *Authors' photo.*

Green Gables Cottage is now the home of Lakeside Women's Club. *Authors' photo.*

Hotel Lakeside is a community landmark that has hosted many notable guests. *Lakeside Association.*

Barberton's Lake Anna was named by Ohio Columbus Barber for his daughter. *Authors' photo.*

A quartet of old movie theaters still stands on Tuscarawas Avenue in Barberton. *Jerrye & Roy Klotz, MD/Wikipedia.*

All that remains of Jaite are ten original buildings, but they are well worth seeing. *Authors' photo.*

The Shaker Heights City Hall is beginning to show its age. *Ford Walker photo.*

These three beautiful homes overlook Green Lake in Shaker Heights. *Spencer/Wikipedia.*

The Mariemont Inn exemplifies the Tudor Revival style that pervades much of the community. *Authors' photo.*

Originally intended for working-class residents, the apartments in Mariemont proved to be too pricey. *Authors' photo.*

The properties in Greenhills were strictly rentals and spartan in appearance. *Authors' photo.*

The Greenhills swimming pool reflects the Art Deco style, as do other public buildings. *Authors' photo.*

cupola on the riverbank at the foot of State Street in Columbus, not far from his plant. Here he lived with his first wife, Alice Booth Hayden, and their children. She passed away in 1865.

In about 1856, a charcoal furnace at Hanging Rock, just outside Ironton, was purchased by the firm of Dille, Brice & Moore. The firm had it dismantled, loaded onto canalboats and relocated to Green Township, just west of Nelsonville, where it was renamed Hocking Furnace. Of all the celebrated Hanging Rock Region blast furnaces, it was located the farthest north. Hayden immediately began buying into the Dille, Brice & Moore until he took sole possession. At the same time, he purchased three thousand acres of land in Green Township, just west of Nelsonville. In the process, he acquired the existing settlement of Hocking Furnace, which was renamed Haydenville.

Peter Hayden chose to put his nephew, Halleck Hayden, in charge of the newly established Haydenville Mining and Manufacturing Company. With his small fleet of canalboats, he supplied coal from the Hocking Valley to his iron foundry in Columbus. However, when deep-bedded fireclays were discovered during coal and iron mining, Hayden began construction of a clay products plant near the railroad depot. He also began hastily constructing wood-frame houses for use by the workers, who flooded the area to work in the lumber, coal, iron, oil and (later) clay industries.

By 1866, Hayden had become president of the Columbus, Hocking Valley & Toledo Railroad, an endeavor he had been instrumental in spearheading. He knew that it would be more efficient to move coal by rail than water. The arrival of the railroad in Haydenville three years later further propelled the opening of other coal mines until by 1890 the population in the region had reached fifteen thousand. The many mining towns that popped up throughout the Hocking Valley became known as the "Little Cities of Black Diamonds." Coal cars regularly pulled onto the tile plant's siding to dump their freight, while passengers boarded at a train station made of the same familiar glazed brick. Before that, the Hocking Valley Canal provided a somewhat slower connection point for coal and other goods, as well as passengers.

One year later, Peter Hayden and his son, William, established P. Hayden & Company, a bank, on Capitol Square in Columbus. The four-story Hayden-Clinton Bank Building, as it has come to be called, still stands across from the statehouse.

While Peter Hayden hoped to make Haydenville the "ideal town," it was much like other company towns in many respects. To begin with, it was owned entirely by the company. All the houses and both of the stores were the property of Haydenville Mining and Manufacturing. In fact, the workers had built not just their own homes but also their church, post office and general store. The workers were paid in company scrip, which was only redeemable at the company stores. No other stores were permitted within the town limits. Many families, including some emancipated slaves, lived in Red Row Hollow close to several mines where they worked. Only employees and their families could live in the houses, and if an employee lost his job, he also lost his home.

Yet Hayden was considered to be more enlightened than many company owners. He earned the respect of his workers—most of them, anyway—and a reputation as a philanthropist. In 1869, for example, he donated five thousand bushels of coal to the Female Benevolent Society and the Hannah Neil Mission, both in Columbus.[175] And in 1877, he and his wife sponsored a Christmas celebration for the families of his employees. The children received gifts beneath a Christmas tree, while the adults feasted on oysters and other delights.

In 1871, Hayden and his second wife, Sarah Barnard Hayden, deeded 1.34 acres of land to the trustees of the Methodist Episcopal Chapel in Haydenville. By this time, he was residing in New York City but still actively engaged in running his businesses. However, despite his reputation for being concerned about his workers, labor strife was unavoidable as the price of coal dropped. During the early months of 1872, Hayden experienced so many strikes that the *Highland Weekly News* reported "he had sent to California to secure one hundred and fifty Chinamen [*sic*] to work his coal mines in Hocking county."[176] However, there is no evidence that this occurred.

Remarkably, in 1877, telephone communications were established between Columbus and Haydenville. During this same period, Peter Hayden was financially backing the construction of the narrow-gauge Paint Valley Railroad, which would allow him to ship coal directly to Cincinnati. However, this route evidently was never completed, possibly because he was losing interest in the coal mining industry.

Starting in 1882, Hayden also manufactured ceramic products, which enabled the community to prosper even as coal mining was being discontinued. He built large kilns to create fine clay products that soon were in demand throughout the country. He put the residents of his company town to work making vitrified ceramic bricks, blocks, tiles, pipes and fittings. They dug clay from the coal and clay mine areas and carted it to the factory using the now-abandoned tunnel through the ridge.

"The factory produced clay building blocks, chimney tops, ceiling tiles, floor arches, partitions, sewer tile, stove pipe, and fire brick," historian May Ann Reeves wrote. "In later years, sidewalk bricks and street paving block with a distinctive circle design were manufactured there as well."[177] Even the two cemeteries in Haydenville contain clay headstones with large, inscribed chimney pots identifying the deceased.

The oldest parts of Haydenville featured row houses crowded along Main Street, all constructed of the same unusually rough, rusty-red brick. The houses varied from two-story dwellings with one wing off to the side to narrow, two-storied saltbox-style houses. Although there were elements of Georgian and Spanish architecture, it was the use of decorative corner quoins, chimney pots and other ceramics produced by the factory that prompted several visiting architecture professors from Ohio University to dub the style "Sewer Pipe Gothic."

The most notable exception to the Haydenville look is the superintendent's house. A wood-frame structure, it was purportedly constructed in Columbus, disassembled and then floated down the Hocking Canal to Haydenville, where it was rebuilt on a hill overlooking the town. There once was a lawn tennis court in front of it.

During the period 1888–93, the Haydenville Methodist Church was built, with the company picking up 90 percent of the expense. "A new Methodist church built of factory-made, rock-faced brick, paving blocks, and various tiles replaced an earlier wood frame church," Reeves related.[178] The striking appearance of the church is due to the use of chipped bricks, hand-chiseled by John Wolfe, and the unexpected use of ceramic pipe for decorative purposes. Large stained-glass windows were contributed by Mrs. Peter Hayden in memory of her late husband, who died before the church was completed. The edifice has changed little during its history.

From 1883 to 1900, Hayden and his nephew became even more creative in using the company's clay sewer pipe, silo tiles and star emblem bricks in the construction of the buildings. There were eighteen round silo tile houses built beside the Hocking River on Hunkey Road (so-called because it was where the Hungarian immigrants lived). Each round house had four rooms, two on the first floor and two more on the second. Only one of these structures remains. According to Reeves, "Other single-family dwellings built during the early twentieth century included two-story, hip-roofed houses with a kitchen or mud room at the rear. The houses continued to be built in a linear development pattern."[179]

Following Peter Hayden's death in 1888 at the age of eighty-two, his body was returned to Columbus for burial at Green Lawn Cemetery. The *Hocking Sentinel* printed a laudatory obituary that described him as

> *one of the most conspicuous men in the modern grown of Columbus, and the heroic pioneer in the development of the Hocking Valley. He acquired great wealth by honest means, applying judgment and vigilance and economy to his business, but was always one of the most liberal and generous men to his employees. During the various troublesome times in the Valley the men in Hayden's employ were faithful to him, contented with the terms of service. His many friends in the Hocking Valley feel keenly the loss sustained in his death.*[180]

The *New York Times* reported that Hayden amassed a fortune in excess of $1 million, enabling him to live on a large scale, including a summer home on Fairyland in the Thousand Islands region of the Saint Lawrence River. His son, Charles, assumed the presidency of the company.

In 1902, the town, the factory and the mines—everything, really—were sold to the National Fire Proofing Company of Pittsburgh for $75,000. Five years later, it would become the National Automatic Tool Company (NATCO). According to Reeves, "Between 1907 and 1914, more houses were built, including some two-story tile duplexes, box-like structures, built to house new Eastern European workers coming to work in the factory on the eve of World War I."[181] There were 115 new wooden houses altogether.

One year later, a brick railroad depot with a tile roof was built in conformance with the requirements of the Hocking Valley Railroad. For many years, the original wooden depot was used as a home. However, it would eventually deteriorate to the point that the decision was made to raze it. The expense of restoring it was more than any of the local nonprofit entities could afford. The hotel will likely be lost as well.

NATCO continued to prosper until World War II, when steel buildings reduced the demand for decorative tile. Consequently, the company converted its production to ceramic conduit before selling out to the National Fireproofing Company. It produced a different type of brick—smoother, as well as more decorative and functional—than had previously been the case.

As Reeves summarized:

> *The company closed Plant No. 1 in 1958; Plant No. 2 followed in 1962. In 1964 NATCO sold the town of Haydenville to* [John Marchetti]

> *an attorney and realtor from Washington, Pennsylvania, for $100,000. The factories and kilns were demolished soon after the purchase. More than a hundred houses were offered for purchase to their current occupants, people who, until then, had been tenants of NATCO. Half were sold to the residents and the balance at public sale.*[182]

The houses were sold for $2,500 to $3,000 each on a land contract.

In 1973, Haydenville was listed in the National Register of Historic Places. The historic district included more than 120 properties spread over twenty acres. However, a half century later, they are rapidly disappearing. The company headquarters, for example, is gone. It housed not only the company offices but also the store, theater and infirmary. So, too, is the railroad station. Of the original 350 row houses, only 122 survive. Altogether, there are 175 homes, but not all are habitable.

Today, Haydenville, population 337, sits as forlorn as a footnote just below SR 33, the main highway through Hocking County. While the Hocking Valley Railway still runs from Nelsonville to Haydenville, it is strictly recreational. The Santa Claus Train is especially popular. Maybe this year he'll have something special in his sack for the town of Haydenville.

Chapter 14

FORT HAYES, 1862

Columbus, Franklin County

"Jazz to Cheer Their Lagging Spirits"

Castles were originally fortifications. So America's castles were the numerous forts that were built during various wars, as well as the country's westward expansion. Since most were built of wood, few have survived. Ohio must have had nearly one hundred of them.

Fort Hayes was a planned community much like all military bases are, and it evolved over time as the uses for it changed. Originally called the Columbus Arsenal, it was created by an act of Congress on July 11, 1862, as a weaponry storage facility for Union troops during the Civil War. Although the Ohio State Arsenal had been completed at 139 West Main Street a year earlier, once the war broke out, the building was so jammed with arms and equipment that the structure was deemed a fire hazard.[183] So the need for a new arsenal was imperative.

General C.P. Buckingham of the Ordnance Corps selected the site of the Columbus Arsenal about 1860. There are still remnants of a Buckingham Street to the east and the west of the property. According to reporter Bill Bush, "The Army began using the site in 1861 but didn't get the deed to the land until 1863, when it purchased the site for $16,000" from Robert and Janette Neil.[184] The population of Columbus was about fifteen thousand at the time.

The proprietors of the Neil House Hotel, the Neils, owned this seventy-acre tract of land located about a half mile northeast of the city. At the

The so-called Shot Tower is the most striking building on the Fort Hayes campus. *Authors' photo.*

time, it was covered with oak trees. The arsenal would be used not only for the receipt, storage and issuance of large quantities arms and equipment but also the manufacture and storage of ammunition. However, the first building wasn't completed until 1864.

Known as No. 62, or the "Shot Tower," it was designed to create cannonballs and other types of ammunition by pouring molten metal into a funnel at the top and allowing it to form ball shapes as it fell through the air before landing in vats of ice water. However, there is some question about whether it was ever actually used for that purpose.

During the following decades, more than one hundred other buildings were constructed, including workshops, storehouses, a stable, a hospital, an officers' club and numerous officers' houses. In addition to the Shot Tower, those still standing include an indoor equestrian arena, gate house, barracks, mess hall, administration building and the general's house.

The first commander of the Columbus Arsenal was Captain J.W. Todd. At the time he took control, the arsenal consisted of little more than a collection of wooden shacks, some of which still remain. Over the years, however, it became the site of many impressive structures. Todd immediately set about developing a plan for the property. The total price tag was $224,075—some $10,000 more than Congress had appropriated. But he wasn't around for its implementation.

In January 1864, Todd was replaced by Captain T.C. Bradford. It was his responsibility to build the post from the ground up. He would remain until 1866, rising to the rank of colonel. Bradford called his operation the "Store House." Although the plans had been drawn up by the Ordnance Corps in Washington, D.C., Bradford instituted many on-site changes as necessity dictated. He obtained sandstone from Newark, brick from Columbus, lumber from southern Ohio and metal cornices from Cincinnati.

Five months later, work started on the officers' quarters and magazine. The latter was designed with a capacity of 2,500 barrels of powder. Soon, the Columbus Arsenal had enough materiel on hand to arm and equip thirty thousand men. In fact, it was also shipping ammunition to two other arsenals. But it wasn't until late in the year that the main building was occupied.

The Columbus Arsenal was completed just as the Civil War was ending. During the last few months of the war, it provided supplies for ten regiments that were being formed at Camp Chase, a prison camp on the far west side of Columbus. "Ironically, the first man killed on the post was a civilian, Nicholas Kaetzel, who, on April 5, 1865 was blown up while firing a salute to honor the capture of Richmond," Virginia, according to the *United States Senate Record*, May 17, 1866.[185]

Not surprisingly, a ghost story developed around Kaetzel's unfortunate demise that was thoroughly debunked by the authors in their book *Columbus State Community College: An Informal History*. While ghost hunters insist that he was a dashing young soldier who was madly in love with the general's daughter and died while firing a salute to honor the recently martyred president, Abraham Lincoln,

> *this story doesn't stand up to scrutiny. To begin with, Kaetzel* [frequently called Hartzell] *was fifty-one years old and married at the time of his death, a little long in the tooth to have captured the heart of the young woman. Furthermore, if the cannon was fired in conjunction with the arrival of Lincoln's funeral train in Columbus, it would have been on April 29, 1865 (not May 16, as some sources claim). However, Nicholas Kaetzel's death actually occurred over three weeks earlier on April 5 or ten days before the President was assassinated!*[186]

For the most part, Colonel Bradford oversaw the business of a largely civilian workforce. It wasn't until October 25, 1865, that the first permanent detachment of enlisted men was stationed there. However, civilian employees continued to repair the Springfield and Enfield rifles by cannibalizing parts. With the end of the war, the arsenal was overflowing with excess ordnance. This resulted in the first public auction of the surplus goods in late November.

In the spring of 1866, Bradford planted $150 worth of shrubs and trees as the first step toward sprucing up the arsenal's appearance. It was his last act before his departure. The facility remained the Columbus Arsenal until September 24, 1875, when it was renamed the Columbus Barracks. It was now used by General Recruiting Service as a depot. The purpose of a military depot is to house and maintain military stores, as well as serve as a reception facility for recruiting and training new soldiers.

As historian Douglas C. McChristian noted, "In fall 1875 the adjutant general named Columbus Barracks in Ohio as a depot for the General Recruiting Service, at the same time ordering training at the temporary Newport subdepot to be discontinued effective April 17, 1876. Like Jefferson Barracks, Columbus would continue to operate as a primary recruit rendezvous and training facility well beyond 1890."[187]

Those receiving training were "specifically music boys, select recruits, disposable recruits, unexamined recruits, and [African American] recruits. Four companies of cadre were organized in February 1881. Recruits were given specialized instruction of from one to four months' duration."[188]

Columbus Barracks also became known for its musicianship. As the Columbus Board of Trade reported in one of its publications, "The recruits and the regular commissioned and non-commissioned officers, together with the famous band, formerly known as the 'Newport Barracks Band,' all under full army discipline, make this an interesting point, and the hospitality of the officers of the post attract hither many of our people and visitors, and add not a little zest and vim to the social life of the city."[189]

However, conditions were not always optimal. In December 1880, a civilian observed that a roll call for 250 recruits required "a quarter of an hour, and is an interesting pastime with the thermometer about 10 deg. below zero."[190] Disease ran rampant, meals were not always adequate and the soldiers sometimes clashed with the denizens of the surrounding neighborhoods. However, training was intense. As one infantry recruit bragged in a letter to his brother, "We have to practice shooting every day that we are not on guard. Firing at 200, 500, and 1200 yards."[191]

When the command general of the Department of the East took over the post, it was garrisoned with the 17th Infantry Regiment. Owing to the Spanish-American War in 1898, more buildings were enlarged, remodeled and constructed to accommodate an increasing number of recruits—including new barracks, a reception center, a drill hall and a bandstand (later moved to the Park of Roses in Clintonville). The post was also enlarged by nearly eight acres. In 1903, it was officially designated the Columbus Recruiting Depot with two infantry companies and six recruiting companies. Located in a parklike setting, it was the largest military recruiting station in the United States by 1915.[192] It also housed the largest government pension office.

With the advent of World War I and the implementation of the Selective Military Conscription Act of 1917 by President Woodrow Wilson, Columbus Barracks became one of the principal induction centers. In particular, many African American enlistees from the southern states were processed through this northern city. The presence of so many southern Black people engendered some resentment among both the white and Black residents of Columbus, setting the progress of civil rights in the city back several decades.

In 1920, Columbus Barracks was designated as the center where recruits who wanted to be in the band would learn to play march music and jazz. In fact, a jazz band often greeted the new recruits to "to cheer their lagging spirits."[193] At the time, the army was in desperate need of musicians. Therefore, band leader Frank J. Weber, later of the St. Louis Symphony, said that any man who could whistle a tune would be taught to play the instrument to which he is best suited. They had two hundred positions to fill.

Two years later, Columbus Barracks was renamed Fort Hayes in honor of former Ohio governor and nineteenth president of the United States Rutherford B. Hayes. Hayes was born just north of Columbus in Delaware. Fort Hayes was now the headquarters of the Fifth Corps Area, comprising the areas of Ohio, West Virginia, Indiana and Kentucky. A decade later, the Civilian Conservation Corps, established by President Frank D. Roosevelt, constructed seven new frame buildings.

With the onset of World War II, Fort Hayes continued to function as a reception center with some 2,000 officers and men stationed on its grounds. "The enlisted men lived in barracks along Cleveland Avenue. Officers lived in 10-room brick houses west of what is now I-71 and I-670," reporter Bernie Karsko wrote.[194] But on March 1, 1944, that function ceased. It was also one of six prisoner of war (POW) camps in Ohio, responsible for holding up to 435 Germans.

At the conclusion of the war, the post was turned over to the Ohio National Guard. "Used by both the Army Reserve and the Guard of Engineers, it continued in use by the State and Federal governments for both military and civilian functions."[195] Then, in 1965, just a century after it was founded, much of Fort Hayes was declared surplus property by the U.S. government and deeded over to the Columbus Public Schools. Five years later, Fort Hayes was listed in the National Register of Historic Places. "At the time it was the oldest military installation in continual use in Ohio," according to Barb Powers of the Ohio Historic Preservation Office.[196]

"In June 1971, the federal government gave 49 acres of the 70-acre base to the Columbus Board of Education," Karsko related.[197] Through the leadership of Jack Gibbs and the efforts of two local congressmen, the Columbus Public Schools system was able to purchase this tract of land for one dollar.

By the 1970s, Fort Hayes had become a facility called the Armed Forces Examining and Entrance Station. There were about 50 soldiers and civilians who commuted to work. Some 150 to 200 recruits per day were processed through a drafty old building called the "Mule Barn." Officially known as Building No. 102, it was built in 1894 and stands seventy-five feet high, with a floor nearly as large as a football field.

Fort Hayes ceased to be an examining and entrance station in 1973. Nathaniel L. Hill, commander of the facility, recalled that the base was like

Many of the Fort Hayes buildings are now used for academic purposes. *Authors' photo.*

a ghost town. While there were still barracks and officers' homes, no one was living in them. Many of these were intentionally burned down as a fire training exercise.

Columbus City Schools opened the Fort Hayes Career Center in 1976 on the grounds of the former military base. "Except for some activity by reservists, the base took on the look of a high school campus."[198] Today, it encompasses three divisions: Fort Hayes Arts and Academic High School, Fort Hayes Career Center and Arts IMPACT Middle School (AIMS). Although several new buildings were constructed to serve the educational needs of the students, several of the old buildings were renovated and repurposed. In the end, less than a score of the original Fort Hayes buildings remain—some preserved, others stabilized and a few in deteriorating condition.

In 1996, the flag of the 83rd Army Command flew for the last time at Fort Hayes. Established in 1967 at Fort Hayes, it had "carried on the tradition of the 83rd Infantry Division, which was organized in 1917 at Camp Sherman near Chillicothe," Felix Hoover reported.[199] But now it had been officially deactivated as part of the army's reduction program. However, its importance as a public educational complex continues to grow.

Chapter 15

DENNISON, 1865

Tuscarawas County

"Dreamsville, Ohio"

When the Pittsburgh, Cincinnati & St. Louis Railway Company announced its intention to make "the principal point on their line between Pittsburgh and Columbus" on the east side of Little Stillwater Creek opposite Uhrichsville, there was no town there.[200] But something similar had happened before. It worked once. Maybe it would work again.

The Ohio & Erie Canal was already in operation when Uhrichsville—named after local mill owner Michael Uhrich—was laid out. And from 1833 to 1850, it experienced a period of rapid growth and prosperity. Wheat buying and shipping was the town's primary business, and flatboats transported surplus grain to markets in the East. This gave rise to the construction of five grain warehouses and a boat building business.

However, the arrival of the railroad in 1850 undercut Uhrichsville's value as a shipping point for grain. Now, a number of smaller stations along the way also engaged in the same enterprise. As a consequence, the town plunged into a period of depression that lasted for about fifteen years. Business slowed to a crawl, property began to depreciate in value and the town grew little if any.

All of that changed when a route was "completed across the Panhandle from Steubenville to Pittsburgh."[201] The managers of the Panhandle route decided that they needed to build some shops midway between Pittsburgh and Columbus. As one county historian took pains to explain,

The Railway Church was built through the efforts of railroad officials and workers. *Authors' photo.*

"The distance to Pittsburgh is ninety-three miles, and to Columbus one hundred, but the grades of the track being considerably greater on the east end rendered the distance equal from an operative standpoint in the minds of the railway officials."[202]

But there were two other factors that influenced their decision. The chosen site had water and coal—water to fill the boilers of the steam engines and coal to fuel the burner. The trains would take on both during their brief stops there.

As soon as the location of the future railroad shops and offices was announced, the Dennison Land Company was formed by a group of ten men, including William Dennison of Columbus. In 1864, the company purchased between four and five hundred acres of land from John Welch Sr., Isaac Osbun and Alex Huston. However, the main portion of Dennison was built on the acreage purchased from Welch.

When the shops were completed the following year, business began booming again in Uhrichsville; nearly overnight, Dennison was born. Named after William Dennison, Ohio's highly regarded governor during the Civil War, the village was laid out in 1865, the same year the shops were completed. The creek was the dividing line between Uhrichsville and Dennison.

Initially, Dennison was dubbed the "Altoona of the Pan Handle road" because it performed the same function that Altoona did for the Pennsylvania Railroad.[203] During the next fifty years, the population rapidly grew from zero to a peak of more than 5,500 people—3,000 of whom worked for the railroad—despite possessing few of the physical attributes to make it a desirable place to live. As one historian noted, "The ground was low, and in some places, swampy, and in wet seasons mud was the most common article to be found on the streets, sidewalks and lots."[204] However, it did possess one advantage that trumped all the drawbacks: good jobs.

The shops of the PC&LRR turned out to be among "the most complete and extensive in the country."[205] They not only repaired existing locomotives and cars for the Pittsburgh to Columbus line but also built new ones and supported the other divisions of the Panhandle system.

While the shops were concentrated on the south side of the track, the north side was dominated by a two-story brick building occupied by the master mechanic's office, train master and telegraph departments. Several smaller buildings housed the offices of the yard dispatcher, superintendent of water works and other ancillary functions. In all, the railroad company occupied forty acres in the center of town, which was bisected nearly in half by the tracks, and employed about seven hundred men year-round.

As J.B. Manfield wrote in 1884, "The whole forms a perfect hive of human industry, and contains some of the finest machinery operated by some of the most skillful mechanics to be found in the world."[206] All passenger trains changed engines when they reached Dennison, and it was also the terminal point for all freight trains. As a result, it came to be the residence of most of the engineers, freight conductors and other railroad men. In 1878, the town was finally incorporated and began annexing additional acreage. The infusion of so much railroad money into Dennison promoted the construction of good streets, substantial business blocks, elegant residences and an unsurpassed system of drainage that had raised it out of marshland.

Early in 1869, "Company Row" occupied nearly all the ground on both sides of South 3rd Street between Bank and Logan. These buildings were owned by the Dennison Land Company and provided housing for many of the railway employees.

The first church built in town, the Dennison Presbyterian Church—commonly known as the "Railway Chapel" (301 Grant Street)—was erected in 1870. Prior to that, some Presbyterian families met in a room in

Benson's Block at the corner of Logan and 1st Streets or in the school. The railroad company—"in their accustomed spirit of generosity"—contributed substantially to the construction of the edifice.

In 1867, there were but three Roman Catholic families in Dennison, but they began to meet once a month in various residences. By 1870, they had commenced building the Church of the Immaculate Conception (206 North 1st Street). It was completed one year later. Future movie star Clark Gable was baptized there.

A ticket, freight and express office was established at Dennison in 1873. Prior to that, all but company business was conducted through the Uhrichsville office. In order to facilitate the delivery of coal, the Dennison Coal Company, which had extensive mining operations just south of town, extended a tramway to the railroad yard just east of the shops.

A large, wood-frame boardinghouse just east of the Railway Hotel, known as the "Big Onion," burned to the ground in 1873. The division superintendent's home also burned down the following year. And four frame buildings behind the depot on Center Street were destroyed by fire in 1881. Each time, Dennison suffered a setback in its growth.

In 1909, postal inspectors discovered that a branch of the Society of the Banana, an extortion ring based in Marion, Ohio, was operating in Dennison, too, in the person of Antonio Viccario.[207] The Society of the Banana was a so-called Black Hand ring, which sent out threatening letters to hundreds of people demanding payment of tribute or they would kill or kidnap them or members of their families. It would be the first gang prosecuted for organized crime in the United States.

During World War II, Dennison was a stop on the National Defense Strategic Railway Route. As the result of the largest mobilization of troops the United State ever witnessed, hundreds of troops began passing through the town on a daily basis. Getting them where they needed to be was of primary importance, but making sure that they were fed fell just below that. Because the stop for water was mandatory for the steam-powered locomotives, the troops would spend five minutes or so gazing out the train window at sleepy little Dennison.

Lucille (Neighbor) Nussdorfer was a pianist, church organist and president of the Fortnightly Music Club and the Twin City Women's Republican Club. When President Herbert Hoover stopped briefly at Dennison on his way to Columbus to give a speech in 1940, she was there to welcome the former president to the station. Her husband, Irvin, was a fireman for the Pennsylvania Railroad.

Lucille purportedly conceived the idea of establishing a canteen after visiting the railroad depot on New Years' Eve 1941 and watching the trainloads of lonely servicemen. "Some were headed east to the European conflict," a reporter later wrote, while "others were going west to the South Pacific."[208] Perhaps Lucille remembered that the Red Cross operated a canteen from a boxcar in Dennison yard to feed and aid troop trains that stopped there. As one volunteer recalled, this was in the era before sliced bread, and she had to make hundreds of sandwiches.

But Lucille didn't do it alone. Recruiting some other women from the community, they raised $200 by putting on a play at Dennison High School. Then, on March 19, 1942, they opened the Dennison canteen in an unused service station directly across the street from the train depot. However, when their money was gone, they asked for assistance from the Salvation Army mission in Dover, some fourteen miles to the northwest. When that organization agreed to be the sponsor, the Pennsylvania Railroad allowed the women to move into the depot's restaurant.

Renamed the Salvation Army Servicemen's Canteen, it was put in the charge of Captain Edward Johnson. Fresh from a three-year hitch in the U.S. Marine Corps, Johnson embraced the idea of assisting other servicemen by means of a railroad canteen.

"Newspapers covered the story," William Ferguson wrote, "and troops as far away as Australia bragged about the women at the Dennison canteen who could serve refreshments to as many as 500 men in 15 minutes. The cheerful volunteers made such an impression that the canteen became nationally known among servicemen and women as 'Dreamsville, Ohio.'"[209]

The nickname "Dreamsville" was said to have been "given to Dennison by a group of grateful Texan soldiers."[210] However, they undoubtedly were inspired by the song "Dreamsville, Ohio," which was copyrighted on October 9, 1941, and popularized by Glenn Miller and others. During their brief stops, the servicemen received sandwiches, doughnuts and paper cups of coffee or milk at the third-largest Salvation Army Canteen in the nation.[211]

> *If you were a soldier, leaving the "farm" for the first time in your life, facing wartime service, feeling afraid and homesick, uncomfortable in a cramped overcrowded train with no air conditioning, and hungry with little or no money—pulling up to what appeared to be small town USA, with pretty girls that reminded you of your mom, your sis, your sweetheart, giving you Free food—it was like a dream come true.*[212]

"At first, the soldiers were unwilling to believe that they were being treated to food, cigarettes or magazines free-of-charge. Many of them didn't leave the train in spite of the invitation," thinking there was a catch.[213] But as news of the Dennison canteen soon spread—boosted by Mayor R.L. "Rabbit" Roby's Home Front public relations office—donations started arriving from people and corporations as far away as New York City and Detroit. Roby would also lead a scrap metal and newspaper drive to keep the canteen open.

The canteen drew volunteers from eight counties—Harrison, Carroll, Holmes, Jefferson, Stark, Coshocton, Guernsey and, of course, Tuscarawas. Some of the volunteers even included their names and addresses on slips of paper hidden in the sandwiches. At least one marriage was known to have resulted. And every region had a volunteer who was responsible for collecting donations, whether money or goods, each month. In short order, the Pennsylvania Railroad began sending word ahead from Steubenville (for westbound trains) and Coshocton (for eastbound) to notify the canteen how many soldiers would be arriving.

For many days following the canteen's launch, Captain Johnson personally supervised the operation. "I was up at 6 o'clock each morning and didn't get to bed until 2:30 the next morning," he recalled.[214] However, he was then transferred to Zanesville, and Adjutant Elizabeth Brooks was assigned to Dennison specifically to oversee the canteen. The Dennison canteen was serving 1,000 to 3,000 soldiers daily—some twenty trains per day. An estimated 1.3 million—13 percent of all armed services personnel—passed through Dennison before it was all over, served by nearly 4,000 volunteers, most of them women. In the case of troop trains, cigarettes and magazines were placed aboard because their destinations were secret.

The Dennison Salvation Army Servicemen's Canteen was in operation from March 19, 1942, through April 8, 1946, at a cost of $1,319,439, with the money raised by volunteers. The last soldier served was John A. Settlemire of Johnstown, Pennsylvania. During its entire run, the canteen neither closed nor ran out of food. Legions of volunteers handed out "thousands of cups of coffee, sandwiches, pies, cakes, cookies, donuts, lollipops, candy bars, pieces of fruit, gum, magazines, and Christmas packages."[215] It was a remarkable morale-building project that turned a small town of 4,500 people into a brief respite for hundreds of thousands of servicemen either on their way to war or returning home.

After the war, however, the demand for the railroad declined as people increasingly relied on cars and trucks. The last passenger train left Dennison in 1968. In the early 1970s, the depot's repair shops—where Samuel Prescott

Bush, father of President George Herbert Walker Bush and grandfather of President George Walker Bush, was once a master mechanic—were closed and removed. The last freight train passed through in 1982.

Fortunately, a grassroots effort led by local townspeople saved the Dennison Train Depot (400 Center Street) from demolition. Instead, it was deeded to the village for $25,000. It is now listed as a National Historic Landmark and the most significant remaining example in the nation of a World War II railroad canteen. Fully restored, the vintage 1873 Depot, which served as the Panhandle Railroad Division Headquarters, houses a museum, restaurant, theater and gift shop. It is the only former railroad building still standing. The attached railroad cars house various exhibits as well as a research library.

Today, there isn't much to see in Dennison, but that's kind of the point. The town rose and fell with the railroad. But what remains is well worth seeing.

Chapter 16

LAKESIDE, 1861

Ottawa County

"The Most American Thing in America"

A visit to Lakeside is like taking a stroll—or, perhaps, riding a bicycle—through a gallery of Norman Rockwell paintings. With a few exceptions, the entire community appears to have been placed under a bell jar just before the Great Depression. Once you pass through the gate, it's as if you've stepped into a time-traveling episode of *The Twilight Zone*.

Lakeside got its start when members of the Methodist Episcopal Church selected an isolated spot on the rocky shore of Marblehead Peninsula as the site for a camp meeting.[216] It was covered with trees and provided an expansive view of Lake Erie. Then, in August 1873, a group of Methodist ministers converged on it with axes and shovels to begin the task of clearing the land. Afterward, they built a podium, some rude benches and stone platforms for bonfires.

"On the edge of the clearing, tents provided shelter for preachers and their families. People from the surrounding countryside arrived on foot and in wagons, for Lakeside's first public event. It was an old-fashioned camp meeting revival with rousing hymns and preachings that matched the surrounding bonfires."[217] At some point, a pier was added to accommodate those who came by boat.

Camp meetings were nothing new in the United States. They had been occurring throughout much of the nineteenth century as a means of bringing religion to thousands of settlers who were living in communities that were

The magnificent Hoover Auditorium was built during the Great Depression. *Lakeside Association.*

not being served by churches. Because many of the attendees had to travel some distance from home, they would camp out near the meeting site.

The Lyceum was another movement during the same period. As early as 1830, Lyceums, named for "ancient Greek self-education groups," began sponsoring lectures, concerts and adult education programs in New England.[218] Following a pause during the Civil War, the Lyceums resumed and began spreading westward, where they reached the shores of New York's Lake Chautauqua. Although not overtly religious, these meetings were driven by the so-called Protestant ethic and focused on self-improvement.

In 1874, two men—Lewis Miller and John Heyl Vincent—founded the New York Chautauqua Assembly on the banks of Lake Chautauqua in rural New York State. Lewis was a successful Ohio businessman and philanthropist who was committed to Sunday school work.[219] Vincent was the director of a Sunday school and, later, a Methodist-Episcopal bishop.[220] According to historian Mary Gasley, "They shared the conviction that religion was worthwhile only as it related to real life."[221] So they developed a program of Bible study, combined with "lectures on history, science, art, geography, and ancient languages."[222] It was a curious blend of the religious and the secular.

The first Chautauqua took place in a wooded grove and was reached by steamship. Significantly, both evangelism and denominationalism were prohibited. As orator T. Dewitt Talmadge declared, "The walls of bigotry have come down."[223] However, the primary intent was educational, and eventually, graduation ceremonies were held and diplomas awarded to those who completed a four-year course of study. And for those who couldn't attend in person, Miller and Vincent created a home reading course—the Chautauqua Literary and Scientific Circles.

With Miller and Vincent's encouragement, the Chautauqua model was soon copied by communities throughout the nation. "Within three years, assemblies were formed in Michigan and Ohio. Inside of a dozen years there were thirty-eight Chautauquas; within two dozen years there were 150."[224] Theodore Roosevelt described the Chautauquas as "the most American thing in America."[225] Nevertheless, there was no formal connection between the various Chautauquas, nor were they ever affiliated with one particular denomination. However, a "sort of mild Protestantism" was the foundation of the Chautauqua movement.[226]

Attendees initially lived in tents, but later some began to build cottages as the two-week program expanded to six with the addition of courses on literature and music. President James A. Garfield—one of the most intellectual of all the commander-in-chiefs—later asserted that "Chautauqua was to show the world how to use leisure."[227] In time, Chautauqua, New York, grew into a town of nearly 5,000 and welcome 100,000 visitors every summer.

Lakeside originated under the sponsorship of the Central Ohio Conference of the Methodist Church. Among those who were instrumental in organizing and financing the Chautauqua were Alexander Clemons, patriarch of one of Marblehead Peninsula's leading families; Reverend Richard P. Duvall, onetime missionary and a local Methodist minister; B.H. Jacobs, Danish immigrant, Civil War veteran and Port Clinton merchant; and Samuel R. Gill, who had grown up on the peninsula.

History records that at the first camp meeting, Reverend Joseph Ayers was chosen as superintendent of the assembly. It is also possible that Lewis Miller, who lived one hundred miles away in Akron, also attended. In the early years, a few cottages were built overlooking Lake Erie, while the number of tents multiplied. Soon the permanent wooden tent frames were transformed into cottages. "Increasing crowds demanded more comfort and in May of 1875 the first unit of the Hotel Lakeside was built."[228]

In retrospect, "[t]he growing Chautauqua Movement was a natural fit for Lakeside. Its first Sunday school training sessions were held in 1877, which blossomed into a robust Chautauqua program full of religion, education, cultural arts and recreation opportunities during the 1890s. Those same four founding elements, or Chautauqua pillars, remain in place at Lakeside Chautauqua today."[229]

"Year after year camp meeting was conducted there," historian Nevin Winter related. "Buildings were erected as the institution demanded, and the grounds were beautified in every way."[230] By 1886, the number of cottages had grown to four hundred or so. One year later, the Lakeside and Marblehead Railroad arrived, providing passenger service directly to the community.

Early on, the Lakeside Association decided that plots of land within the one-square-mile community would not be sold outright, but rather would be offered on renewable ninety-nine-year leases. An architectural historian has written, "Lakeside's eclectic Victorian-era cottages are similar in scale and character: they are predominately narrow, 2-story, front-gabled dwellings with prominent porches and balconies. Stylistically, however, they vary greatly in their Italianate, Gothic Revival, Second Empire, and Queen Anne decorative details."[231]

At the same time, Lakeside began to erect a series of Mission-style community buildings. "These include the 1921 Lakeside Administration Building, 1928 Orchestra Hall, and 1929 Hoover Auditorium. A small commercial district also developed near the north end of the property at the intersection of Second and Walnut streets."[232] Today, there are nine hundred cottages and nearly fifty commercial buildings. As a result, the entire village of Lakeside is listed in the National Register of Historic Places.

Although Lakeside's waterfront pavilion has been reconstructed on several occasions, each time an effort was made to retain its original nineteenth-century look. According to historian Peter Ketter, "Buildings from the second half of the twentieth century are relatively few and are scattered throughout the community. As a result, Lakeside still closely resembles its overall appearance before 1930."[233]

Many famous people have made an appearance at Lakeside. In 1879, future president William McKinley, then a U.S. congressman, moved the Grand Army of the Republic reunions to Lakeside in order to prevent them from turning into "drunken brawls."[234] Intoxicating beverages are not sold at Lakeside. For that reason, the reunions would remain there for the next quarter of a century.

While making a speech at Lakeside in 1895, women's rights crusader Susan B. Anthony fainted on the podium. Early reports were that she had died. Some newspapers even published stories about her demise, which Anthony was said to have enjoyed reading.

In 1920, pioneering social worker Jane Addams, an activist for peace during World War I, spoke on "World Food and World Politics." Among the many other notable speakers who have appeared at Lakeside are First Lady Eleanor Roosevelt, sports executive Branch Rickey, retailer J.C. Penney and adventurer Lowell Thomas.

Aviatrix Amelia Earhart spoke at Lakeside twice, in 1934 and 1935, but disappeared in 1937 along with copilot Fred Noonan during a flight from Hawaii to Australia just five weeks before she was scheduled for a return engagement.

Starting in 1927, jazz great Jimmie Lunceford and a band of his music students developed his signature sound during summer engagements at Lakeside. "Dr. Crow, a Memphis physician, whose children were Lunceford's students, owned a dance hall in Lakeside, Ohio, and invited the school band to entertain his clientele."[235] Two years later, they turned professional. Other musical entertainers have included Ray Charles, Victor Borge, Eileen Farrell, Melissa Manchester, Amy Grant, Al Stewart, Chubby Checker, David Cassidy, America, the Guess Who, the Turtles and the Lakeside Symphony Orchestra.

Although Lakeside has roughly 600 year-round residents, the population swells to 3,000 during the summer, not counting the 150,000 visitors. From mid-June through Labor Day weekend, there is an admission charge to enter the gated community and another to attend the many scheduled events.

Occasional fires over the years have altered the appearance of Lakeside, but only marginally. In 1905, a fire broke out in the Carroll Brothers' General Store that consumed an entire block before it was contained. Another in 1929 destroyed the Methodist Episcopal church. Still other fires have burned up to eight cottages or other structures at a time. In nearly all instances, they were quickly rebuilt much as they were before.

The Victorian-era Hotel Lakeside (150 Maple Avenue) was built in 1874, opened for business a year later and was enlarged in 1879 and 1890. President Rutherford B. Hayes stayed there when he attended the reunions of his Civil War regiment, the 23rd Ohio Volunteer Infantry.

Heritage Hall (238 Maple Avenue) is the Lakeside Heritage Society's local history museum, dedicated to telling the fascinating stories of the community. The museum is housed in the original Methodist Episcopal Chapel, which was built in 1875.

Built as the German Auditorium, South Auditorium (540 Central Avenue), as it is now called, was used by German-speaking Methodists from 1883 to 1933. It was then repurposed for youth conferences and various other events.

Bradley Temple (215 Cedar Avenue) was constructed by Mrs. Helen Bradley in 1887 and dedicated to the memory of her husband, Captain Alva Bradley (Thomas Alva Edison was named after him). The building was intended to be used for children's programming, including Sunday school. In her will, Mrs. Bradley stipulated that if it ever ceased to be used for that purpose, ownership would revert back to the Bradley family.

The recently opened Slack House (236 Walnut Avenue) Historic Café occupied a multi-room building that was known as the Slack House from 1891 to 1961. According to Chef Stacy Maple, "It was like a modern-day mall. It had a doctor's office, room and board, and a cafeteria where people gathered to eat."[236] Unlike other restaurants in Lakeside, the Slack House planned to operate year-round. However, it recently closed.

The Epworth Lodge was constructed in 1919 for use by the Epworth League (Methodist youth groups). In 1999, it became the C. Kirk Rhein Jr. Center for the Living Arts (125 West 6th Street).

Construction on the Arthur L. Hoover Auditorium (115 West 3rd Street) began in 1929. Originally called Central Auditorium, it is named after Lakeside's onetime general manager. After construction came to a halt as a result of the Great Depression, the project was completed through a donation by the Hoover family. Patriarch Isaac W. Hoover had invented the Hoover Potato Digger. With a seating capacity of three thousand persons, Hoover Auditorium is used for worship services on Sunday mornings and headline events during the week.

Orchestra Hall (236 Walnut Street) is the only movie theater in Ottawa County. Built in 1927, it was designed in the Colonial Renaissance style. It offers movies as well as live performances.

There are numerous "cottages"—some rather large—to admire, many with interesting histories. The Norton-Scott Home (308 Lakefront Drive) is a pre-Lakeside farmhouse and, as such, has a deed rather than a lease. It was once owned by a wealthy but secretive antiques dealer who purportedly kept her son locked in his room at night to keep him from consorting with another Lakeside youth.

The Gregg-Granstaff Cottage (350 Maple Avenue) was built in about 1875 by two families from Lorain, Ohio. They arrived by sailboat and built what was deemed by one historian "a rambling old barn."[237] This changed in 1927 when the building was cut apart and made into separate cottages.

The Maxwell House (239 Walnut Avenue) was built in 1886 and served as the Lakeside Post Office from 1910 to 1922. It has been owned by just three families.

The Keystone Cottage (202 Maple Avenue), built in 1888, is the oldest cottage in continuous use as a guest house in Lakeside, having provided sleeping accommodations for more than 120 years under the management of just four owners.

Dating back to 1891, the Reade Robertson House (404 East 3rd Street) was once owned by William Gamble, the son of James Gamble of the Proctor & Gamble Company. It was later occupied by a countess.

"By the early 1900s, more than 300 Chautauqua-style resorts associated with various Christian and Jewish congregations had been established from New Jersey to California."[238] More than a century later, just two of the original Chautauquas have survived: Chautauqua Lake, New York, and Lakeside, Ohio. However, the movement is experiencing something of a revival, and more than a score have popped up around the country.

Chapter 17

BARBERTON, 1891

Summit County

The "Magic City"

With a name like Ohio Columbus Barber (1841–1920), this Akron industrialist's parents clearly expected great things of him. And he did not disappoint. During the fifteen years following the Civil War, he built his father's modest, kitchen-based match company into one of the largest in the United States. Then, in 1881, he began consolidating with other match companies—eleven in all—under the Diamond Match Corporation banner. It was called Diamond Match Corporation because the match sticks were diamond-shaped.

"Starting with a block of wood," Molly Gase related in her profile of Barber, "the individual splints were cut into the shape of a diamond."[239] However, it has also been suggested that the name was taken from Diamond State Parlor Matches, one of companies Barber purchased.

Before long, Barber, a giant of a man at over six and a half feet tall, was the undisputed Match King of America with 85 percent of the market. Although he was a major figure in his hometown of Akron, serving first as the president of the First National Bank and later as the president of the combined First and Second National Banks, he still wasn't satisfied. Having decided to also produce match boxes, he formed the New Portage Strawboard Company in 1882.

Barber believed that the perfect location for his new factory would be in the village of New Portage, five miles outside Akron. It was on the Ohio

The Piggery is one of many repurposed Anna Dean Farms buildings. *Authors' photo.*

Canal with a connection to the Cleveland, Akron & Columbus and the New York, Pennsylvania & Ohio Railroads. Not surprisingly, its biggest customer would be his own Diamond Match Company.

In January 1890, Barber and three Akron businessmen—attorney Charles Beard, hardware merchant Albert T. Paige and Barber's best friend, brother-in-law and company treasurer, John K. Robinson—purchased nearly 550 acres of farmland to the west of the Tuscarawas River. Their plan was to establish a new manufacturing center because Akron was becoming overcrowded.

"Barber had become familiar with the work of M.J. Alexander, a Pennsylvania man who had developed what was called a 'magic formula' for turning farm land into thriving industrial communities," a town history notes.[240] Alexander had transformed Jeannette and Charleroi, Pennsylvania, into boomtowns by recruiting industries to move there, which then created a demand for housing and services. Those who purchased lots in these towns saw their property values escalate as the communities grew and additional industries arrived.

The Barberton Land and Improvement Company, as the men called their development corporation, then hired William A. Johnston, also of Pennsylvania, to design the town. "Utilizing a natural glacial lake as its focal point, Barberton's founders laid out streets and lots for an attractive community of homes, churches, schools, and commercial buildings, and established many of the industries required to sustain it."[241]

Lake Anna—named for Barber's daughter, Anna Laura—was transformed into a twenty-acre park in the center of the Barberton. A natural kettle lake spanning ten acres and 828 feet in diameter, it formed when a large chunk of ice broke off a glacier and melted some fifteen thousand years ago. "The surrounding 203 acres were subdivided into building lots, spreading back evenly from the lake on all sides, with a small extension to the north to connect the town with the State Road (Norton Avenue)."[242] In the span of one year, a community of nearly two thousand people was built from the ground up.

In promoting Barberton, the land company emphasized its beautiful setting:

> *The sparkling lake, the undulating land the forest-clad hills in the distance on every hand form a panorama of rare beauty. Around the lake will be a park of some extent. From the streets fronting the lake the town extent evenly back to the Belt Line. Fronting the lake will be the Barberton Inn, intended to be the best hotel in the Western Reserve.*[243]

Although Barber and his associates were determined to ensure that their ventured turned a profit, they realized that they needed to strike a healthy balance between the needs of industry and commerce and the desire for healthy and quiet residential neighborhoods. Toward that end, Barber broke ground for his own National Sewer Piper Company.

"Thought to be the largest manufacturer of its kind, the company was producing 200 tons of sewer pipe and employing 150 people by the end of 1891."[244] But he did not stop there. He also established four more companies: Creedmore Cartridge, Barberton Whiteware, American Alumina and Stirling Boiler. To these were added Kirkum Art Tile and the United States Company.

Early in 1891, the Belt Line Railroad was also under construction, and Barber opened the town's first bank, the Barberton Savings Bank. In order to house the workers, National Sewer Piper built thirty small cottages and a hotel and Stirling Boiler another ten houses. By the end of the year, more than three hundred homes had been constructed. A nine-block-long business district was taking shape, with the earliest businesses concentrated at the corners.

Benjamin F. Tracy, a buyer for the Strawboard factory, built the Tracy Block on Tuscarawas Avenue. It was soon joined by the Moor and St. John Block. Two of the surviving structures are a tailor's house (219 2nd Street NW) and a druggist's (220 2nd Street NW).

The Barberton Land and Improvement Company set aside a full block for the Barberton Inn. Opened in 1895 as the finest luxury hotel in northern Ohio, it was so successful that an annex had to be built five years later. However, it became unprofitable in about 1905 due to its inability to compete with hotels in Akron. Ten years later, it was sold and razed, although the annex was adapted for use as the Barberton City Hall.

When the population of Barberton reached 1,300, it was incorporated as a village, enabling it to establish a school system and various municipal services. Barberton's growth was so amazing that a newspaper reporter called it magical, which was how Barberton became known as the "Magic City." But then the town got caught up in the economic Panic of 1893, forcing several businesses to close. In order to prop up the local economy, Barber decided to move the Diamond Match Works from Akron to Barberton. Within two years, more than two thousand men and women were working at the new Diamond Match plant. Soon he was producing 250 million matches per day.

In 1894, Barber founded the Diamond Rubber Company with the help of a chemist named Arthur Marks. "When Barber sold his company to BF Goodrich in 1912, he became a multi-millionaire," according to local historian Bernie Gnap.[245] "Barber's instincts drove him to search for solutions to problems in his factories," Molly Gase observed. Because some of his businesses used flammable materials, he worked on developing better fire extinguishers. And when he discovered that the use of phosphorous in the match-making process caused a disease called phosphorus necrosis, or "phossy jaw," he implemented dental clinics for his employees so they could receive treatment.

Although he kept physically fit and personally believed that he would live to be one hundred, Barber was shocked when his longtime friend John Robinson passed away in 1908. Barber had retired three years earlier, but he now turned his attention to building his dream home—a fifty-two-room French Renaissance Revival–style mansion on a hill east of town. He also constructed an experimental farm with thirty-five buildings in the same architectural style. He called the complex Anna Dean Farm, now listed in the National Register of Historic Places. While Barber's hope was to establish an agricultural college, he died in 1920 before he could do so. The mansion was later razed, but nine of the farm building survive.

Constructed in 1909, Barn Number One (3rd Street SE and Portsmouth Avenue) was the first cattle barn built on the Anna Dean Farm. Although it is now the largest remaining building at twenty-five thousand square feet, it was the smallest of the three main cow barns. Built in 1912 at a cost of $50,000, the brick-and-mortar Piggery (248 East Robinson Avenue) was the last building Barber erected for Anna Dean Farm. Although constructed for Berkshire swine, it later housed Dorset sheep. It is now a special event center.

The Heating House (360 East Robinson Avenue) provided heating for five acres of greenhouses via its 1911 Stirling boiler. It is one of three known sets of Stirling boilers built by Babcock & Wilcox remaining in the United States. The Creamery (Portsmouth near 3rd Street SE) was where Anna Dean Farm milk and ice cream was packaged. Built in 1909, it is now a private residence.

Although it resembles a two-story house, the Poultry Manager's Office (139 2nd Street SE) was where all the business of the Anna Dean Poultry Department was conducted. Located behind the Poultry Manager's Office, the Feed Barn dates back to 1910 and is the only building on the Anna Dean Farm constructed of smooth-faced brown concrete block with cut sandstone sills. The Feed Barn was used to store and dispense feed to the farm's chickens and ducks.

The Brooder Barn (112 2nd Street SE) served as a chicken coop from 1910 until 1920 and once housed the world's largest incubator. The second-floor apartment was occupied by the barn manager and his family. The Colt Barn (740 Austin Drive) was built in 1910. Originally intended for bulls, it is the smallest of the remaining major barns on the Anna Dean Farm.

From 1910 to 1920, the population of Barberton doubled to 18,811. In 1911, it was proclaimed a city. Many of the new residents came from eastern Europe, but some also relocated from elsewhere in Ohio or adjoining states. As Barberton grew, it annexed the neighborhoods of North, East, South and West Barberton.

Other historic sites include the O.C. Barber Dam. Located on Conservatory Drive behind the Anna Dean Retail Center, it was constructed in 1910 and restored in 2001. It is 160 feet long and privately owned. Near the Robinson Avenue Bridge is an Ohio Canal Slip, one of the few still in existence. A slip was a wide place in a canal where two boats and their mules could pass each other.

The Diamond Machine Complex (2nd Street and Wooster Road West) contains the remnants of the Victorian-era buildings that house the match-making machinery plant of Diamond Match Company. They date back to 1894 and are some of the oldest remaining industrial buildings in Summit County.

The Belt Line Railroad yards are also in this area. The railroad was an important component of Barber's plan for the town, providing the local industries with access to the major railroads. The Erie Depot (361 4th Street NW) was built in 1890 by Barber and restored by the Barberton Historical Society. Presidents Theodore Roosevelt and William Howard Taft made campaign stops there, while President Warren G. Harding's funeral train also stopped. The town also was connected to Akron by streetcar, providing its citizens with easy access to business enterprises in the larger city.

The three-story Tracy Block (4th Street and Tuscarawas Avenue) was built in 1891 and is the oldest surviving brick building in downtown Barberton. Incorporating elements of Victorian Gothic in its design, it is listed in the National Register of Historic Places, as are a number of other buildings in the downtown. The high school was once on the top floor, the city government on the second and the jail in the basement.

The four-story Weisberger Company department store (553–57 Tuscarawas Avenue West) was built in 1928. With a parapet façade and central nameplate typical of the period, it was Barberton's first large-scale department store and was in continuous operation for more than sixty years. Central Savings and Trust (523–25 Tuscarawas Avenue West), built in 1918, is Barberton's only remaining early bank building. Its monumental Neoclassical character is seen in its stone façade, two-story Corinthian columns and decorative roofline treatment.

A quartet of early movie theaters still stand on Tuscarawas Avenue. Gem Theater (528 Tuscarawas Avenue West) is the oldest of a trio of early silent movie houses in Barberton, dating back to 1910. The Park Theatre (565–69 West Tuscarawas Avenue) was built in 1919 to show silent movies. It boasts a richly decorated façade of brick, terra-cotta and tile in a Neoclassical Revival style. A Page organ was installed in 1926, and eventually sound films were shown there. It was renovated in 2000. Located practically next door, the Pastime Theater (559 Tuscarawas Avenue West) is just two years younger and features a sparkling white-glazed terra-cotta façade, also Neoclassical. Lake Theater (578-588 Tuscarawas Avenue West) is an Art Deco–style movie house built during the Great Depression. William Henry operated a café in the building (524 Tuscarawas Avenue West) from about 1905 to 1920. He lived in one of the apartments above it. A recent renovation restored much of its original appearance.

Second Avenue also has a wealth of early buildings. K's Kandies (176 2nd Street NW) was built in 1893 or so as a free-standing structure. It was both commercial and residential. The Italianate Bevard Block (219 2nd Street NW) was built in 1891, the year of Barberton's founding. The Finnel & Smith Agency has occupied it for more than half of its existence. The Frase and Sherrard Drug Store (220–26 2nd Street NW) was built in two stages, 1891 and 1900. A drugstore in the corner storefront survived for almost a century. The Welker Building (229–31 2nd Street NW) was constructed by Alvin Welker. The north half housed his grocery business and the south half his residence. It dates from 1891–1901.

Several examples of Queen Anne–style residential architecture still stand at 123 and 221 3rd Street and 571 Lake Avenue. They are characterized by turrets, varied rooflines, decorative patterns on gables and bay windows. During the early 1900s, the architecture became more restrained, reflecting the Colonial Revival style. There are several notable examples at 308 and 416 6th Street and 191 3rd Street. They are identifiable by their classical columns and front gables with brackets.

Today, Barberton is a city in search of an identity. While much of its past is still on display, you have to know where to look and what you are looking at. Someday, perhaps, it will find its magic again.

Chapter 18

JAITE, 1906

Cuyahoga/Summit Counties

"Away from the Hustle and Bustle"

Born in Breslau, Germany in 1859, Charles H. Jaite (1859–1931) immigrated to Cleveland with his parents the following year. At the age of thirteen, he ended his formal education and went to work in a paper mill. An ambitious youth, Charles "set out to master every detail of the business, and in time became a thorough expert."[246] In 1880, at the age of twenty-one, he became a naturalized citizen after renouncing all allegiance and fidelity to Emperor William II.

Charles married Edith Clara Peebles of Cuyahoga Falls. They had six children—four daughters and two sons, one of whom died in childhood. Eventually, Charles rose to the presidency of the Standard Bag & Paper Company, while also serving as vice-president of the Cleveland Paper Company.

When these two firms merged to form the Cleveland-Akron Bag Company in 1902, Charles was placed in "charge of the manufacturing part of the business, and located the plant in Boston Township, Summit County."[247] Three years later, he resigned as director and manager and sold all of his stock, having decided that he wanted to start his own papermaking enterprise.

On September 18, 1905, Charles founded the Jaite Company, which was incorporated with $100,000 of capital stock. He installed himself as president; his brothers Robert H. Jaite and Emil W. Jaite as vice-president

The Jaite Company Store is now the Cuyahoga Valley National Park Headquarters. *Authors' photo.*

and secretary, respectively; and his brother-in-law Julius Kreckel as treasurer. The partners purchased more than twenty-two acres in the Cuyahoga Valley. Some eighty acres constituted the farm of Reverend Lathrop Cooley, a former missionary and shrewd investor whose widow would leave "approximately $100,000 for the establishment of a hospital in East Cleveland to be known as the Lathrop Cooley Memorial hospital."[248]

The men set about hiring local farmers to construct the building that would house the mill. Sand was dredged from the nearby Cuyahoga River to manufacture concrete block to use in constructing the buildings needed for the plant. Tracks were then laid to connect the mill to the Ohio & Erie Canal and Cleveland Terminal & Valley Railroad. The Cuyahoga Valley railroad had completed its line through the area in 1880. "The crossroads that became 'Jaite' initially was called 'Vaughn Station,' after the Vaughan Family who settled the area in the 1940s (the 'a' was dropped)."[249] Before 1900, Vaughn's siding was a shipping point for log timbers.

The partners also drilled six wells, five gas wells to power the plant—although they proved to be problematic—and one artesian well to supply water. The water was of such "purity that the paper manufactured with its use is many points stronger than paper made…with ordinary water."[250]

"The machine room of the plant is 50 by 200 feet in dimensions," a history of Summit County noted, "and over this, in the second story, is located the bag factory."[251] At the time of construction, the plant was capable of manufacturing eight tons of paper a day, which was then made into paper sacks that were sold directly to flour mills and cement plants. Initially, the mills produced the sacks from recycled rags and ropes.

From the beginning, Charles envisioned creating not just a paper mill, but a community. In 1906, he bought land on Riverview Road, where he had five two-story buildings constructed to house employees in a rural section near Brecksville. A decade later, he added four small single-family units on Vaughn Road. This was the nucleus of a company town that would grow to include other homes, a general store, a post office and a railroad station. However, Charles never compelled his employees to live in the housing he provided, nor did he pay them in company scrip. He also endeavored to keep things affordable.

Jaite's policy of paying his employees in hard cash apparently did not go unnoticed. On September 9, 1926, Charles Jaite and Julius Kreckel, company treasurer, were held up by four masked men armed with shotguns and revolvers as they were returning from Cleveland with the company payroll. "Messrs. Kreckle [*sic*], Jaite and the driver [Fred Weldy] of their automobile were bound and gagged and left in bushes near the plant."[252] The thieves made off with $8,400. Several men were later arrested for the crime.

Jaite Paper Company was ideally located, halfway between Cleveland and Akron on relatively cheap land. The first product produced was Blue Line Paper. Manufactured on a cylinder machine, it was used for flour sacks. "In those first years, after an eight to ten hour day, workers were expected to stay after and mix cement and sand to make more blocks to expand the factory."[253] In 1908, the Jaite Company was considered by William B. Doyle, in his *Centennial History of Summit County*, "one of the most important business enterprises of this section of Summit County.'"[254] But it was also dangerous work.

On November 2, 1910, "Walter Zaninski [aka Zemansky] and George Bollock, workmen at the Jaite paper mill…were torn to pieces and killed by being caught in the shafting of the mill…when they went into the basement to adjust a belt."[255] The story was widely circulated, but it was not all that uncommon for the era. Men were often maimed, if not killed, by machines. Five years later, when the quarries in nearby Peninsula shut down for an indefinite period of time, Jaite Paper Company quickly hired a number of the laid-off workers.

Prior to the First World War, Jaite purchased all of the kraft pulp used in the manufacture of bag paper specialties from Brown Corporation.

However, "soon after the war broke out the products of the Brown mills were commandeered by the British government and it was then that C.H. Jaite started to make his own pulp and build a recovery furnace."[256] Instead of using the customary evaporating system, Jaite used natural gas to speed up the process—a novel idea at the time. About the same time, the company "purchased a car to convey its women employees to and from the mill."[257] Nearly all of the workers lived in the communities of Boston, Peninsula or Jaite.[258]

"By 1918, 214 employees worked at Jaite Mill, and by the Depression years, nearly 250 people were employed. A third of these were women who sewed the bags and worked in the offices."[259] When a second cylinder machine was added, Jaite Paper began producing fertilizer bags and bread sacks. In 1926, a few of the cylinder machines were converted into two Fourdrinier machines. They could produce continuous rolls of paper with several layers for strength. Two years later, the company produced its first successful multi-walled cement bag. These would be advertised as "Jaite Puncture and Waterproof Bags."

At its height during the 1920s and 1930s, Jaite Paper was the eleventh-largest multi-wall paper manufacturing company in the nation. During the Depression, the mill operated twenty-four hours a day, providing jobs not only for the local community but also for the many Polish immigrants who moved there. Not surprisingly, it felt like a family because many of them were. "In a University of Akron interview, Willy Ritch recalled, 'Everybody was related to one another…in the bag plant: father, mother, daughter, son, brothers, sisters.'"[260]

According to Bertha Jones, who was born in Jaite but grew up in Peninsula, "Those houses there at Jaite were mostly habituated [*sic*] by people from foreign extraction, and they had German, Polish, Hungarian. And the smells that came from all those houses were all different."[261]

Josephine Davis, who lived in nearby Brecksville and was a secretary at the Jaite Paper Company, considered it to be a good place to work. All of her sisters worked there until they married. Her brothers were involved in making and inspecting the bags, but one of them was the chauffeur full time. She recalled that "one of the Jaites took us to a show at the Palace [in Cleveland]," Josephine recalled. "And I remember that it was Vaudeville and girls dancing.…[T]hat's the first show I ever saw."[262]

When production was at its peak, workers slept in shifts in the dormitory. Others walked to work or were transported by the company from the towns of Boston or Peninsula. Four times a day, the company whistle sounded, announcing shift changes. As Jerry Cervenski observed, "It was an enjoyable place to work…away from the hustle and bustle of everything."[263]

In 1928, Jaite Company announced that it would be opening a plant in St. Helens, Oregon. Apparently, the demand for its products was exceeding the capacity of the existing plant. But it is also likely that Charles wanted to manufacture his products closer to where the demand was. The success of the Jaite paper mill, historian William Doyle asserted, "must be attributed to the quiet, resourceful man who studied the manufacture of paper in a practical way from boyhood."[264]

Charles was always known to be fairly private individual, as well as a civic-minded individual and a good Methodist. When he passed away in 1931, he was succeeded by his son, Roy Jaite. Although Robert "Pop" Jaite was still associated with the company, he was seventy-one years old and spent much of his time racing his speedboat.[265]

Four years later, Roy built a second paper bag factory on the West Coast, this one in Wilmington, California. After visiting the home office in Ohio, Gus Bauman, manager of the Wilmington branch, reported that business conditions were more favorable in California than the Midwest. During the 1940s, the company advertised that it was manufacturing its multiwall paper bags "for defense sand bags, cement, lime, plaster, fertilizers and manures, chemicals, asphalt, rotary mud, grains, feeds and other products requiring protection and strength."[266] They even developed a paper stretcher and a paper sleeping bag for use by the army.

As a small, privately owned mill, Jaite Paper Company was no longer able to compete with larger mills following World War II, especially those in the South. So, in 1951, the Jaite family sold the mill to the National Container Corporation, and the company whistle fell silent. The company would change hands several more times after that before it eventually closed in 1984. However, in 1975, the National Park Service stepped in. Four years later, the Jaite Mill Historic District was listed in the National Register of Historic Places. The next year, NPS purchased the property, including the company town. They were rehabilitated for use as the park headquarters and painted a distinctive yellow color.

Although the NPS contemplated adapting the industrial buildings for new uses, arsonists struck on October 2, 1992, rendering the mill dangerous and, ultimately, unsalvageable. At that point, the goal shifted to "rehabilitating the mill site and restoring natural habitat."[267] Nearly $11.5 million was appropriated by the federal government for the demolition of the building and the restoration of the site. An original 1928 Fourdrinier machine was retained to explain how the mill turned pulp into paper, and corner markers were put in place to denote the extent of the mill.

Since the paper mill was razed, the community of Jaite Mill consists of ten buildings: a couple of two-family Managers' Houses, built in 1906; a combination Post Office and General Store with a second-floor apartment for the store manager and his family; four Worker's Houses built in 1917; and the Jaite Depot, Freight Station and Privy. All of the homes were occupied up until they were acquired by the National Park Service.

There was originally a row of five Managers' Houses on Riverview Road, all duplexes of similar appearance, but three of them burned down. The four single-family Worker's Houses on Vaughn Road are also of identical bungalow design but differ in decorative detailing. The Depot was still being used as a railroad operating point to relay messages until the job was abolished in the late 1970s. And the Company Store served as a church for a time before being converted into apartments. According to Charles's grandson, all of the houses and the store were originally painted white. They are now a distinctive yellow.

Chapter 19

SHAKER HEIGHTS, 1911

Cuyahoga County

"The Pot of Gold at the Rainbow's End"

There are no Shakers in Shaker Heights. But before there was a Shaker Heights, there was a Shaker settlement called North Union. The communal society was founded by Ralph Russell, who had come from Connecticut preaching the doctrine of the United Society of Believers in Christ's Second Coming to anyone who would listen. Russell had been inspired by a visit to the Shaker settlement of Union Village in Lebanon, Ohio. Soon thereafter, he converted his wife and more than thirty members of his family to his newfound faith.

Ann Lee, an illiterate English factory worker, founded the sect in about 1747. She believed that she was the second coming of Jesus Christ and taught her followers that they should live pure and perfect lives in "the kingdom come." Called "Shakers" because of their propensity for ecstatic dancing during their religious services, they would prove to be the most enduring of all the American utopian experiments. Among their most distinctive practices were total equality between men and women, communal ownership of property and abstinence from marriage and sexual relations. In 1774, Mother Ann and eight of her acolytes came to the British colonies to spread her new gospel in the New World. After she died in 1784, her followers founded the United Society of Believers, also known as the Millennial Church.

With just over eighty converts, Ralph Russell established a Shaker community in 1822 on one thousand acres of land just six miles southeast

There are a wide variety of mansions scattered throughout Shaker Heights. *Authors' photo.*

of Cleveland in Cuyahoga County. It was an area they referred to as the "Valley of God's Pleasure," despite not being a valley at all. Between 1826 and 1854, they built dams across Doan Brook, forming Upper and Lower Lake. They also erected three gristmills and a sawmill, while increasing their numbers to some three hundred members.

Since the Shakers practiced celibacy, they were dependent on new recruits if they were going to prosper. But North Union had ceased to grow by 1850, and Russell renounced his membership in the faith. When the number of Shakers dropped to twenty-seven, the decision was made to disband in 1889. The property was initially sold to a land development company in Buffalo, New York, but eventually was acquired by a couple of brothers named Van Sweringen.

Oris Paxton and Mantis James Van Sweringen were railroad barons who also engaged in land speculation. They were as peculiar in their own way as the Shakers had been in theirs. The brothers never married, shared a bedroom in their fifty-four-room mansion and seldom appeared in public except together. When they secured options on some 1,400 acres of land formerly owned by the North Union Community of the Society of Believes, "the Vans," as they were known, planned to create a garden community reminiscent of Baltimore's Roland Park. It would be a suburban retreat for wealthy Clevelanders.

The Van Sweringen brothers named their creation Shaker Heights in recognition of its Shaker heritage and its location on a piece of ground several hundred feet above Cleveland. "Of all of Cleveland's suburbs," historian George Condon wrote, "Shaker Heights easily is the most famous—and least known."[268] To facilitate their vision, they constructed an interurban streetcar line—the Shaker Heights Rapid Transit—from Public Square in downtown Cleveland to Shaker Square, recognized as the second planned shopping center in the United States.

"The national image projected by Shaker Heights," Condon observed, "is one of extreme prosperity and, appropriately enough, utopian living. The irony is that it started out to be a spiritual Utopia and came to be a materialistic paradise; a communistic experiment turned into a capitalistic triumph."[269] Shaker Heights would prove to be "the largest and wealthiest real estate subdivision in the United States."[270]

In concept, Shaker Heights was about as far removed from the Shaker community that preceded it as possible. "The idea, simply, was to build a terribly expensive, terribly exclusive, terribly desirable suburb."[271] Like other garden communities, the typical grid plan was jettisoned in favor of curving boulevards, broad avenues and beautiful homes—no two alike—on sweeping lawns in a majestic parklike setting. They would even exercise approval over the buyers in order to keep undesirables out.

Incorporated in 1911, Shaker Village, as it was originally called, was not an immediate success. The problem was the lack of public transportation linking the suburb with downtown Cleveland. Earlier, the Vans had dealt with a similar problem by striking a deal with the Cleveland Railway Company to extend service to Cleveland Heights. However, the president of the company felt that he had been burned by that deal and was reluctant to enter into another. So at Oris's suggestion, he and his brother decided to build their own using a natural ravine, Kinsgbury Run. They called their venture the Cleveland & Youngstown Railroad Company. It was to be a high-speed commuter service reaching speeds of up to fifty miles per hour as it made the trip from Public Square to Shaker Square and back again.

Next the Vans tackled the problem of replacing the old railroad depot with something more fitting the well-dressed businessmen who would be making the daily commute from Shaker Heights. Although it took several years, they eventually got their wish and the new Union Terminal was built. In the process, many of Cleveland's most historic buildings were razed, as well as a good number of eyesores and three cemeteries—all in the name of progress.

According to Condon, "From 1919 to 1929, Shaker Heights added, on the average, 300 new, expensive homes each year."[272] During that decade, the suburb's population increased from 1,700 to 15,500. The value of the property increased by a factor of 80. Their personal worth was $100 million. And then the stock market crashed. By this time, their main source of income was the investments they held in a number of railroads. These fell off precipitously. The sale of real estate, which had brought in $5.6 million in 1926, dropped to $65,000 eight years later. By 1935, they were $73 million in the red. A few months after, Mantis died. The following year, Oris joined him. Most agreed that he hadn't been the same since his older brother passed away.

Like most developers of their era, Oris and Mantis did not envision a community that included non-whites and non-Protestants. "The Van Sweringen Company," Chethan Chandra has written, "emphasized its ideals through a series of ads in an old newspaper called the *Cleveland Topics*. 'On every family's horizon is a rainbow,' read one ad, 'and for many the pot of gold at the rainbow's end is Shaker Village.'"[273]

However, during the period of 1910–20, the African American population of Cleveland increased more than 300 percent. Although Cleveland had been on a progressive trajectory up until that point when it came to civil rights, historian Kenneth L Kusmer noted that there was a "sharp increase in racial tension and institutional discrimination in Cleveland to 1915 because of the Great Migration."[274] A 1925 editorial in *Cleveland Topics* made its position clear: "These southern negroes are not welcome here. Please do not delude yourself, or delude them."[275] The same held true for many of Ohio's larger population centers. Consequently, segregation—which had been waning—returned.

"By 1930, approximately 1,200 Black domestic servants lived and worked for white employers in Shaker. Some of these servants' children were even allowed to attend Shaker schools. But Shaker Heights was largely too expensive and hostile for Black homeowners," Chandra related.[276] It would have taken an exceptional man of color to purchase a home in Shaker Heights, but Dr. E.A. Bailey, an African American physician, did just that in 1925. And it did not go unnoticed. As Russell H. Davis wrote in *Black Americans in Cleveland*, "Dr. Bailey reported that shortly after occupying the home, bricks were thrown and shots were fired at his home and an attempted was made to set fire to his garage."[277]

Predictably, perhaps, the police were less a help than a hindrance, and Bailey was forced to move. Furthermore, some four hundred property owners in Shaker Heights banded to together to form the Committee of the Shaker Heights Protective Association. Working in concert with the Van Sweringen Company, the property owners passed a series of restrictions that effectively precluded African Americans from buying houses in Shaker Heights. It was only after the U.S. Supreme Court struck down such deed restrictions that wealthier Black professionals began moving into Shaker Heights.

In 1986, the City of Shaker Heights established a Fund for the Future of Shaker Heights. Its purpose was to make loans available "for down payments for residents buying homes in segregated neighborhoods, creating multi-ethnic neighborhoods."[278] Presumably, the Shakers, if not the Van Sweringen brothers, would have approved.

Today, Shaker Heights is roughly 55 percent white and 36 percent Black, with a median household income of $92,463. The average home value is $272,597. It's likely that Oris and Mantis Van Sweringen would be astounded by this transformation in their suburban dreamland, but others view it as progress, though, possibly, not enough. It hasn't been too many years since one *Cleveland Plain Dealer* reader referred to the residents as "the 'progressive,' snooty, pseudo-intellectual limousine liberal, socialists of Shaker Heights."[279]

Although none of the Shaker buildings remain, some 280 acres of park lands were donated to the City of Cleveland in 1892. The Shaker Historical Museum houses furniture and other artifacts from Shaker communities and interprets the history. However, much remains of the Vans' planned community. Roughly 75 percent of it is listed in the National Register of Historic Places as the Shaker Village Historic District. Tours of Shaker Heights often focus on the creations of specific architects. The city's Landmark Commission provides a number of online maps for this purpose.

Architect Bloodgood Tuttle designed thirty-six homes in the village, including two groups of "demonstration homes." The purpose of the demonstration homes was to illustrate the types of houses and materials that would be appropriate to early Shaker Heights. Constructed in 1924, one group of five was built on Van Aken Boulevard near Southington Road and another group of four near Parkland Drive. Although he died in Cleveland in about 1936, little is known about Tuttle's life.

A Cleveland native, Charles S. Schneider is most famous for his design of Stan Hywet Hall, the Akron residence of the Seiberling family. He was also responsible for a 1928 Georgian home called Temple of the Winds, an in-town country estate on South Park Boulevard in Shaker Heights, as well as Shaker Heights City Hall in 1929.

Harry L. Shupe was a native of Shiloh, Ohio, and later was sent to Cleveland to attend Central High School. When Shupe designed homes for Shaker Heights, he adhered to the Vans' strict building codes. All of his homes were in the English and Colonial styles, although he aspired to give each one its unique character. Altogether, he designed more than sixty-three homes in Cleveland Heights and Shaker Heights between 1915 and 1930.

Born in Philadelphia, Monroe W. Copper Jr. designed two thousand houses in thirteen states, including one hundred in Shaker Heights. He also designed fifty-nine churches, as well as many restaurants, office buildings, hospitals and even condominiums. With so much work in the Midwest, he eventually settled in Gates Mills, Ohio. For Shaker Heights, Copper created homes in all three of the approved styles—English, Colonial and French.

Howell & Thomas (Carl Eugene Howell and James William Thomas Jr.) was already known as a leading architectural firm for larger homes when it became involved with Shaker Heights. From roughly 1915 to 1930, the partners were responsible for several dozen impressive homes in both Cleveland Heights and Shaker Heights. Formed in Columbus, where they are best remembered for their design of East High School, they then switched their focus to Cleveland following World War I. In Shaker Heights, they designed a group of four English homes at Shaker and Courtland Boulevards and seven model homes along Parkland Drive. They also covered all three approved styles.

The firm of Small & Rowley (Philip Small and Charles Rowley) focused on Colonial and English Revival designs. Founded in 1921, the firm closed in 1928 due to Small's taking a full-time position with the Van Sweringens. They were responsible for remodeling the farm buildings to create Daisy Hill, the Vans' mansion in Hunting Valley. While Small designed a group of five demonstration homes in Shaker Heights on or near South Woodland Road, Rowley designed the Shaker Heights Main Library.

Shaker Heights consists of nine different neighborhoods, each named after one of the nine original elementary schools: Boulevard, Fernway, Lomond, Ludlow, Malvern, Mercer, Moreland, Onaway and Sussex. While there are literally thousands of houses in the community, those west of Warrensville Center Road reflect the strict architectural guidelines established by the Van Sweringen Company. It's a great place to just wander around.

Chapter 20

MARIEMONT, 1923

Hamilton County

"The First Planned Garden Suburb"

In *City Life*, his classic book on the life and death of American cities, architectural historian Witold Rybczynski identified Mariemont in Hamilton County as the nation's first planned garden suburb. "It was," he wrote, the work of "an enlightened developer, Mary M. Emery, who wanted to create a model community that would demonstrate the value of modern (that is, Garden City) planning ideas."[280]

Toward that end, Mary hired renowned city planner John Nolen, who was joined by more than two dozen leading American architects in creating a planned community ten miles east of downtown Cincinnati. It would be reminiscent of an English garden city.

"Starting from scratch on 420 acres, Nolen created a formal town center focused on a village green and bisected by a boulevard avenue, with streets radiating out into the village," Rybczynski noted. "The plan is an extraordinarily subtle exercise in axial formalism combined with a very relaxed form of grid planning, which is all the more impressive when one appreciates this is among the first suburbs planned expressly for the automobiles."[281]

So, who was Mary Emery? According to preservationist Maya Drozda, "In 1866, Mary Muhlenberg married Thomas J. Emery, the son of a prominent local entrepreneur. His and his brother John's company, Thomas Emery's Sons, developed real estate throughout Cincinnati, leaving their

Mariemont was modeled after an English garden community. *Authors' photo.*

distinctive mark on many neighborhoods that initially developed as streetcar suburbs."[282]

Mary and Thomas Emery had two sons, Sheldon and Albert. Sadly, Albert died in an accident in 1884, while Sheldon succumbed to pneumonia six years later. Although the Emerys owned a mansion known as Edgecliff, which overlooked the Ohio River, they also bought an enormous mansion, Mariemont, near Newport, Rhode Island. The couple undoubtedly planned to live out their retirement years there together.

However, in 1906, Thomas passed away while on a business trip to Egypt, leaving Mary an estate worth $20 million (the equivalent of about $660 million in today's dollars). For decades afterward, Mary mourned the deaths of her husband and sons, all while donating her fortune to worthy causes. Among them were the YMCA, the Cincinnati Zoo, the Emery Theatre and various hospitals and colleges. But she was also involved in a larger but less public enterprise.

For some fifteen years, Mary had quietly purchased land from thirty different property owners, keeping her identity hidden so no one would catch wind of what she was doing and thereby drive the prices up. In all, she spent more than $7 million developing a community that she would name Mariemont. She intended it "as an antidote to the urban housing conditions of major American cities in the early 20th century."[283] Ideally, it was to be "an affordable community, and it included a variety of lot sizes, as well as low-rise apartment buildings and commercial buildings with flats above stores."[284]

It is believed that there were three distinct early Indian village sites scattered over the Mariemont property. "Ten mounds, in addition to two circular earthworks, were found. They were called 'Fort Ancient Sites,' and definitely tie into the pre-historic occupation of the entire southwestern part of Ohio," historian Warren Wright Parks noted.[285] Unfortunately, as the land was developed, all of these mounds, which stood five to seven feet high, were leveled. But a five-acre plot of land called the Madisonville Site has been preserved on a bluff above the Little Miami River.

"A visitor to Mariemont's site in the early 1920s," historian Millard F. Rogers Jr. wrote, "traveling on…U.S. Route 50, a two-lane highway, saw only cornfields, and patches of vegetables grown on acreage dotted with a few farmhouses. One narrow road intersected the highway near an architectural landmark, the Ferris house, built shortly after 1800."[286] The Eliphalet Ferris House would be restored as a museum. Several other existing homes were moved.

The choice of John Nolen as the town planner was not surprising, given the magnitude of the project. He was widely regarded as the best in his profession. According to Parks, "During the thirty years of his professional life as a landscape architect and city and regional planner, he was engaged on more than four hundred public planning projects."[287] Each architectural firm was specifically invited to participate in creating Mariemont. Charles J. Livingood, the project manager, did not dictate the housing style to the architects, "but he expected a harmonious relationship to other buildings in the area."[288]

Groundbreaking took place on April 25, 1923, with Mary Emery turning the first spade of earth. She was seventy-eight years old. She would die four years later. The creation of Mariemont involved more than building apartments and houses. It entailed developing an industrial district to be called Westover where a number of factories would be built, providing employment opportunities for the residents of Mariemont. The first to be constructed were Fountain Way Washing, Searchlight Mirror, Wholesale Petroleum Products Company, Ilsco Copper Tube, the Cincinnati Gear Company plant and a facility for the U.S. Army Corps of Engineers.

There was also the matter of utilities. Mariemont had to arrange for its citizens to have access to water, sewers, drains, natural gas, electrical power and telephone service. These were addressed in various and sometimes novel ways. In order to maintain the look of an English garden city, the decision was made to bury all of the gas, power and telephone lines. They even built a District Heating System for part of the town.

Residential construction did not start until April 1, 1924, when excavation began for the Dana Apartment at the northwest corner of Plainville Road and Chestnut Street. Named after the architect Richard H. Dana of New York, an authority on Colonial architecture, it consisted of a sixteen-family apartment building and thirty group houses, all of brick. On April 24, the groundbreaking was held for Dale Park School, which was designed by the Cincinnati architectural firm of (Lincoln) Fechheimer, (Benjamin) Ihorst and (P.L.) McCoy to match the look of the Dana Group. Although born deaf, Fechheimer was the principal architect of the group.

One month after construction began on the Dana Group, the Ripley Group was started. The architects were Hubert G. Ripley and Addison B. LeBoutillier of Boston. Located on the northeast and northwest corners of Oak and Chestnut Streets, they consisted of three-story apartments with stores on the ground level to form a "Little Town Center."[289] The initial occupants were Kroger, Schlueter's Dry Goods, Fenton, Model Laundry, a delicatessen and a barbershop. They were soon followed by a Central Trust Company branch and a drugstore. A row of sixteen group houses on the lane just east of Beech Street were also part of the Ripley Group.

At about the same time, an apartment building on Beech Street and Murray Avenue and thirteen group houses on the east side of Beech Street—all designed by Clinton MacKenzie of New York—were also being built. All made of stone and stucco, they constituted the MacKenzie Group.

Thirty-one brick group houses on the west side of Beech Street were the contribution of Charles F. Cellarious of Cincinnati. The Cellarious Group "extended from a point south of Elm Street to a point opposite the Mackenzie Apartment."[290] Some were so-called St. Louis Flats, with one apartment above instead of beside the other. Cellarious also designed the original fire/police station. Preservationist Maya Drozda described it as having "the appearance of a fairytale cottage in Tudor Revival style of brick and half-timber construction with a slate roof and small dormer window protruding above the porch."[291] It now houses offices.

The Kruckemeyer & Strong Group were the products of Cincinnati architects Edward H. Kruckemeyer and Charles R. Strong. These frame and stucco houses line Maple Street—twenty-four on the north side and twenty-three on the south. They are characterized by "gable roofs with brown shingles, light tan/cream stucco, and small entry porches."[292] A service lane encircles them so that Maple Street is free of delivery traffic.

Robert R. McGoodwin of Philadelphia designed twelve six-room brick houses—three of which were doubles—on Albert Place on the southeast side of Miami Road opposite West Street. The McGoodwin Group has a private lane surrounding it faced by attached garages.

Another Cincinnati architect, Charles W. Short Jr., was responsible for the Short Group. It comprises three single-family houses and one two-family home, all constructed of stone. They are located on the west side of Oak Street across from the church.

In July 1924, construction begin on the Gilchrist Group. Designed by F.B. Gilchrist of Philadelphia, these thirty-nine homes in Georgian Revival style show "how the so-called 'Philadelphia Row' may be broken into pleasing units by varying setbacks and irregular roof lines."[293] They are located along Plainville Road, rounding the corner onto Murray Avenue with six of the units extending west of Oak Street.

Eight stucco group homes on the south side of Chestnut Street between Beech and Oak constitute the Ziegler Group. They were designed by Philadelphia's Carl A. Ziegler.

The Howe & Manning Group was the work of two female architects from Boston—Lois Lilly Howe and Eleanor Manning O'Connor. It was the second architectural firm in the United States founded by women, with an emphasis on domestic architecture. They designed eight group homes on the south side of Chestnut Street, between Beech and Oak Streets. Because women architects were generally limited to residential projects, Howe & Manning adopted the slogan "the woman's touch in architecture."[294]

Oscar Elzner and George M. Anderson of Cincinnati designed a dozen single-family cottages on Linden Place and the south side of Wooster Park west of Beech Street. These homes in the Elzner & Anderson Group shared a community garage.

Ten Elizabethan homes of timbered stone and stucco were designed by Grosvenor Atterbury of New York. The Atterbury Group was constructed on Sheldon Close, just outside Dale Park.

John Zettel and Walter L. Rapp of Cincinnati designed the iconic Mariemont Inn on the northwest corner of Town Center. Located in the middle of town, the V-shaped structure was originally intended to have longer wings so that the hotel wouldn't dominate the structure. However, economic realities conspired against that plan. The Mariemont Inn overlooks the Town Center Fountain where six roads converge. An adjoining block houses the Mariemont Theatre. Built by a third party in 1938, the 725-seat movie palace opened on Christmas Day. There are other businesses flanking it on either side.

Of all the structures erected in Mariemont, Memorial Church represents the strongest commitment to the English garden city concept. Designed by Canadian-born New York architect Louis F. Jallade, it is in the English Norman style and was inspired by the Stoke-Poges Church near Windsor. In choosing a location for the church, it seemed natural to place it on a rise of ground containing the existing pioneer cemetery and not far removed from the center of town. While traveling through Britain, Jallade learned that in Calcot the stone roof of one of the oldest tithe barns in England had collapsed. "This barn had once belonged to the Cistercian Monks of Kingswood Abbey" and dated back to 1300.[295] So, he bought the stone and used it for the church roof.

Similarly, the hand-hewn beams used to support the roof were obtained from an old mill that was located in the pioneering community of Columbia, which was located on a stream near the Little Miami River. And the bronze bell that hangs in the church was obtained from Athens, Greece, where it had hung in the belfry of an old Byzantine church. Although many of the buildings in Mariemont appear to be older than they are, nowhere else reflects the same attention to detail as the Memorial Church, save the Lich Gate. This simple structure, open on both ends, provides a passage through the stone wall to the cemetery.

Other highlights of a trip to Mariemont include the stone Concourse and wooden Pergola, the rustic stone Boat House and Norman Gothic Revival Carillon Tower in Dogwood Park, Mariemont High School and the limestone Statuary Group in Dale Park.

Not surprisingly, various structures are scattered around the fringes of Mariemont that were not part of Mariemont proper. One of these was Mariemont Hospital (later St. Theresa), which was begun in 1924 "where the lowlands met the higher elevations of Indian Hill, a suburb of multiacre estates that developed about the same time as Mrs. Emery's now town."[296] The design was not out of keeping with Mariemont's other public buildings. The hospital was later converted to a nursing home.

However, Mary Emery's dream of welcoming all classes was not accomplished. As construction costs rose, so did apartment rents and the price of new homes. Furthermore, the Emerys' "compassionate interest and long record…in support of African-American causes" was thwarted by deed and land contract restrictions that prohibited non-whites from living in Mariemont except as house servants.[297] This may have also included Roman Catholics. As a promotional brochure asserted, lots "may be assigned to anyone acceptable, like yourself, to the company."[298] There was no doubt what that meant. Today, Mariemont remains about 94 percent white, with an average home value of $447,981 and a median household income of $104,828.

Chapter 21

GREENHILLS, 1938

Hamilton County

"Pioneering a Dream"

On April 1, 1938, the first residents moved to Avenell Lane in the village of Greenhills, Ohio, but it was no April Fools' joke. Greenhills was a greenbelt community, one of three built by the federal government under President Franklin D. Roosevelt's New Deal social program. The other two were Greenbelt, Maryland, and Greendale, Wisconsin. They were called "greenbelt" communities because they would be ringed by a "green belt" of undeveloped land. Although the short-lived Resettlement Administration "planned to build 25 cooperative towns surrounded by greenspace of forests and farmland," it ran out of funds after Greendale was completed.[299]

These greenbelt communities were the brainchild of former Columbia University economics professor Rexford Tugwell. Often branded a Socialist, Tugwell stated, "My idea is to go just outside centers of population, pick up cheap land, build a whole community and entice people into it, then go back into the cities and tear down whole slums and make parks of them."[300] The Roosevelt administration also saw them as a good make-work project. However, after the Resettlement Administration was declared unconstitutional by a federal court, the rehabilitation of urban slums would have to wait.

More than one hundred cities were considered for greenbelt towns, including St. Louis, Missouri, and Trenton, New Jersey. However, Trenton's Homestead community was never completed due to legal wrangling over the program, and the St. Louis community was dropped completely.

The Greenhills Community Building is decorated inside with WPA murals. *Authors' photo.*

Greenhills was intended to be sort of a working-class utopia, providing affordable housing in a bucolic environment. But the word itself—*utopia*—means nowhere, and Greenhills inevitably fell short of its goal, despite a cost of $11.5 million.[301] It began with the purchase of 5,360 acres of land in Springfield Township, about thirteen miles north of Cincinnati in Hamilton County. Most of the landowners readily sold their plots, except for a farmer named Bastion, who wanted nothing to do with the government. He allegedly shot at federal agents who trespassed on his land.

According to reporter Jeff Suess, "About 3,300 workers spent 4.3 million man-hours constructing the town, and many of them became its first residents."[302] One of them was Nick Bates. Hired as a construction supervisor, he rode his mule to work every day from his home (a tent) in Mount Healthy. He eventually settled in Greenhills, becoming the village's maintenance supervisor and heading the volunteer fire department.

Professor Julie Turner, who has extensively researched the Greenhills communities, noted, "The towns specifically addressed many of the anxieties of the era between the World Wars: fears about urbanization, about the 'machine age,' about changing family dynamics and gender roles, etc."[303] The planners provided swimming pools and movie theaters "to bolster the idea of a traditional American way of life" through encouraging neighborly interactions.[304]

"Planners Justin Hartzog [an Ohio native], who also helped plan Mariemont, and William Strong had the roads follow the natural rolling topography, with housing on dead-end side streets to cut down on traffic and make it safer for children to play."[305] As Alex Baca noted, Hartzog drew his inspiration from the "Garden City concept of British theorist Ebenezer Howard" and "subdivided the village into roughly circular 'superblocks.'"[306]

"The community was organized into neighborhood sections with letters A through F applied to all street names," according to preservationist Beth Sullebarger. "Each section has a mix of dwellings, one or more collector streets, a series of cul-de-sacs or short lanes, pedestrian paths, parks, playgrounds, and public green spaces such as commons or planted median strips."[307] The intent was to have narrow streets with no four-way intersections for safety.

The buildings themselves were a mix of Colonial Revival to Moderne (Art Deco) and International Style modernism, utilizing a range of materials that included brick, stucco, concrete block and even asbestos-cement lap siding. As a result, Greenhills gives the appearance of having been built over many years rather than all at once. In the tradition of a self-contained village, an effort was made to provide the residents with everything they would need in one convenient location. A shopping center—one of Ohio's earliest strip malls—was also constructed, and a community building housed a library, gym and motion picture facility.

A total of 676 dwellings was completed, reduced from 1,000 due to budget cuts. Most of them were flat-roofed apartments or multifamily townhouses, although a few stand-alone homes also dotted the village. Many of them faced "backwards," looking out onto parks rather than the streets. However, none of them could be purchased outright. They all were rented at an average rate of $27.62 per month. To qualify, a renter had to earn between $1,000 and $2,500 per year. While this prevented many lower-income families from applying, those who exceeded the income cap—which was checked annually—would be asked to leave.

English professor Mary Ellen Seery's family qualified. They moved to Greenhills in 1938, and she was born there in 1941. As she recalled years later:

> *This was a godsend for a lot of people....I think my family was very typical in that way. They were ecstatic they got on the list. They talked about that all their lives, how important it was at that point of their lives, during the Depression, for a young couple to move into a glorious place with all these other young couples. They made lots of friends in the community.*[308]

Seery also remembered lots of "get-togethers and potlucking with other families"—the sort of activities Tugwell wanted to promote.[309] However, due to the community's isolation from the outside world, her parents decided to send her to Our Lady of Angels Catholic School in Saint Bernard rather than Greenhills High School. Not only did it broaden her horizons, but she also got to know Black students from the West End.

Another artifact of the times was the inclusion of murals, sculpture and other artwork produced by the Works Progress Administration (WPA). For example, the community building boasts a series of large murals by Richard Zoellner, Leo Murphy and Paul Chidlaw that can still be seen in the library, cafeteria and second-floor music room. And a ceramic bas-relief titled *Community Life*, created by Whitney Atchley, hangs above the stage in the gymnasium.

Like the other "FDR Towns," Greenhills was both a planned community and a "sundown town"—that is to say, it included restrictive covenants in the leases to prevent minorities from occupying the homes. Although President Roosevelt had banned discrimination based on race, creed, color or national origin when it came to hiring by the government, the Federal Housing Administration justified excluding non-whites by claiming that African Americans and other people of color would cause property values to plummet. Author Richard Rothstein in *The Color of Law* asserted that "the housing programs begun under the New Deal were tantamount to a 'state-sponsored system of segregation'" and continue to have repercussions today.[310]

Although they were not permitted to live there, Bloys Parrish and Clarence Paige, two African American men, were employed as janitors in the school. Paige was a noted saxophonist and bandleader who worked in Greenhills from the late 1940s to the mid-1960s, commuting from his home in Cincinnati's West End. Bobbe Kugele, who was born in Greenhills, recalled, "The thing is, those were the only black people I ever saw until I got my first job."[311]

The government also divided up the land north of Greenhills into large farms so the residents of the village could purchase produce and dairy products locally. The forest to the south of the village was deeded over to Hamilton County to form Winton Woods, a large outdoor recreation area.

Following World War II, however, the federal government decided to put an end to the greenbelt experiment, despite having added more single-family homes for military veterans. On December 9, 1949, the Greenhills Home Owners Corporation—a nonprofit group formed by the tenants—

purchased 610 acres of the community for $3.5 million. The tenants were then given the opportunity to purchase the dwellings they had previously been renting. In addition, the "northern farmland was sold in 1952 to create New Greenhills, which was instead named Forest Park."[312]

During the intervening years, some aspects of the original village have begun to disappear. For example, fifty-two of the original flat-roof apartments were razed in 2009 after years of neglect, despite the fact that they had been listed in the National Register of Historic Places along with the rest of the community. Another group of properties was demolished in 2017 due to insurmountable problems, including asbestos, mold, foundation collapse and worn-out boilers. And more are likely to fall despite the pride that many residents take in their historic community.

"Everyone agrees that Greenhills' early intentional planning, and the social consciousness imbued in its physical layout, housing stock, and public art, makes it special and worth preserving," Alex Baca observed.[313] But that comes at a steep cost. Today, many of the residents of Greenhills are the descendants of the original pioneering families, hence the community's motto, "Pioneering a Dream."

Jackie Noble was two years old when her parents moved to Greenhills in 1938. She has resided there almost continuously ever since. "I don't know if Eleanor Roosevelt [an early champion of the program] expected this or not," she told writer Nick Swartsell. "But she had to sit back and think, 'I did a good thing.' Of course it worked. It's still working. My granddaughter and great-granddaughter are still living in the village. That's five generations."[314]

But Greenhills could not remain an insulated community forever. In August 1963, at about 9:30 in the evening, fifteen-year-old Patty Rebholz started walking home from a dance at the town's American Legion Hall. She never arrived. "After a frenzied search, police found her at 5:30 a.m., strangled and beaten to death, in the backyard of a house across the street from where her boyfriend, 15-year old Mike Wehrung, lived."[315] Nothing like that had ever happened in Greenhills before. Although Wehrung was suspected, Benjamin Schwartz, a juvenile court judge, stepped in, made Wehrung a ward of the state and shipped him off to a North Carolina military school. When he eventually stood trial in 2000, a jury found him not guilty, "in part due to a lost deposition from 1963 in which a witness placed Wehrung in his own living room at the time of the murder."[316]

Nevertheless, the damage had been done. The community was so shaken by the murder of Patty Rebholz that people began locking their doors, and the neighborly feel began to slip away. Many didn't feel safe anymore. It was no longer the idyllic setting it had once been. "I still see a lot of the old times here," Jackie Noble said. "But I don't think there is the same openness that there used to be. How do you explain it? People aren't as secluded out here now. We were secluded, we knew it, but we didn't think about it that way."[317]

The first people of color moved into Greenhills between 1960 and 1970, when the census showed ten individuals. They weren't necessarily welcomed. Then, in the 1970s, the National Association for the Advancement of Colored People (NAACP) sued Greenhills and a number of other local school districts in order to force them to integrate. As a result, more than one hundred Black students from Forest Park were bused to Greenhills in 1979. For Kathy Y. Wilson, one of the students, this experience helped launch her career as a writer. While she endured some troubling incidents, she didn't experience the degree of racial tension that she expected. Nevertheless, "It ignited me. It really did. And everything that goes along with it, even teaching, I think I got that from Greenhills."[318] Now, about one-fifth of the residents are people of color.

However, not everyone agrees that Greenhills is a success. According to Sullebarger, one big reason is this: "When the greenbelt communities were being planned, the original goal was to create towns that would have 25,000 units in them and, instead, because the budget was cut, they took it down to 5,000, and I think only 1,600 were built."[319] Because it has such a small residential tax base, there is little that the community can do without government assistance.

There is still much to see in Greenhills. The Art Deco swimming pool and community center and the clusters of attached houses and apartment buildings "hint at Greenhills' significance as a radical social experiment of the New Deal."[320] And there's its reputation as being a Mayberry sort of place. But it may not be enough to save it in the long run.

Afterword

INTERRUPTED DREAMS

There are many other communities we could and maybe should have written about but didn't. And every one of them began with a dream. It could be one person's dream or the shared dream of a group of people. Take Lincoln Village. Located on the west side of Columbus in Franklin County, Lincoln Village is generally dismissed as just another housing development, but it didn't start out that way. Murray Lincoln's dream for it was much more ambitious.

Born in Raynham, Massachusetts, Murray Lincoln (1892–1966) grew up on a small farm. After obtaining an undergraduate degree from the Massachusetts Agricultural College, he launched a highly successful career that resulted in his being hired as the first executive vice-president of the Ohio Farm Bureau. He was fond of saying that every big organization needs a "vice president in charge of revolution."[321] Murray felt that his role was to shake things up. With the support of the U.S. Cooperative Movement, he had promoted the cooperative ideology to Ohio farmers as a response to Communism. The cooperative would provide a counterbalance to unrestrained private enterprise.

At the same time, Murray became the founder of Farm Bureau Mutual Insurance Company, which evolved into Nationwide Insurance. Then, in 1939, he was elected president of the companies, serving in that capacity until his retirement in 1964. Not long after assuming the presidency, he began thinking about building a suburban village—a self-contained model city with affordable housing. Westinghouse had just built a large plant in Columbus, and it needed affordable housing for its employees. But the company did not want to be both a landlord and employer. So it turned to real estate developer and sportsman John W. Galbreath for help. And Galbreath turned to Murray. Because there was a shortage of housing during the post–World War II era, Murray decided to see what he could do to address that need.

With several successful ventures (co-op and not) under his belt, Murray was able to finance the development of Lincoln Village by drawing on the assets from these corporations, but primarily the Farm Bureau Mutual Insurance Company. He founded the People's Development Corporation as a subsidiary to construct Lincoln Village at a projected cost of $30 million. Designed to provide housing for ten thousand residents, Lincoln Village encompassed some 1,120 acres in total and was centered on a nearly 20-acre civic center. Construction began in 1953 and would include 750 apartments, 900 single-family homes, a school, a library, playgrounds, wooded parks, a fire station and churches. The houses were purportedly priced from $9,000 to $16,000, although a Honeywell ad in *Life* magazine listed the range as $12,250 to $27,500.

"People who understand housing values," Murray said, "tell me that there is more value per dollar in Lincoln Village than there is for any other new house for sale at the same price."[322] But it was not easy to see, and he feared that the unscrupulous builder would cut corners while constructing similar-looking homes. He was also frustrated by the fact that he had difficulty showing the prospective buyer what a great value a Lincoln Village home was.

The first residents of Lincoln Village were the John Smitherman family. His wife became membership chairman of a newly formed Welcome Wagon club. Although Murray envisioned his creation as a self-governing city, it never was. His dream was never fully realized, possibly because architect Carl Frye, vice-president and general manager for the development, died before it was completed.[323]

Nearly seventy-five years later, few people recall the origins of Lincoln Village. To most, it's just another subdivision in a city that has its share. Murray Lincoln barely mentioned it in his autobiography. However, as recently as 2021, Lincoln Village was named the sixth-hottest housing market in the nation by Realtor.com—or at least the 43228 ZIP code was. The primary reason was its affordability. In that sense, Murray Lincoln's dream, albeit slightly tarnished, continues.

So remember: an abandoned building you drive by every day may have been the setting for an amazing story that is in danger of being forgotten.

The house you live in may have been home to some truly remarkable people. Or the mound of earth in a remote field may be the remnants of an ancient earthwork. History doesn't happen somewhere else. Once upon a time, Ohio was the Wild West. And before that, Ohio was the site of an incredible civilization. There is evidence everywhere. You just have to know where to look and take the time to do it.

NOTES

Introduction

1. There is also evidence that Ohio was visited by Paleoindians some thirteen thousand years ago—eight thousand years before the pyramids were built.
2. Despite what you might have learned in history class, La Salle never claimed that he did.
3. Since author Sherman Alexie of the Spokane-Couer d'Alene tribe has said that he prefers the term "Indians" to "Native Americans," we use both.
4. Gershon, "Yes, Americans Owned Land Before Columbus."
5. Ibid.
6. Walton, "Forgotten History of Ohio's Indigenous Peoples."
7. Ibid.
8. Worthington Memory, "Brief History of Bill Moose."
9. Hatcher, *Western Reserve*.

Chapter 1

10. This is roughly from when Leif Erikson settled in Canada until the population of the Thirteen Colonies reached 1.5 million.
11. Aloia, "Archaeology as Restoration."
12. Thomas, *Exploring Ancient Native America*.

13. Gibbon, *Archaeology of Prehistoric Native American.*
14. Thomas, *Exploring Ancient Native America.*
15. McLeod, *Astronomy in the Ancient World.*
16. McManamon, *Archaeology in America.*
17. Thomas, *Exploring Ancient Native America.*
18. Reitz, *Case Studies in Environmental Archaeology.*

Chapter 2

19. Moravians are United Brethren, a German-speaking Protestant denomination that predates the Lutherans by a century.
20. Zepp, "By the Beautiful Spring."
21. Manfield, *History of Tuscarawas County.*
22. Zepp, "By the Beautiful Spring."
23. Robinson, "First Christian Indian Church."
24. Zepp, "By the Beautiful Spring."
25. Ibid.
26. Ibid.
27. Kornwolf, *Architecture and Town Planning.*
28. Ibid.
29. Jackson, *Century of Dishonor.*
30. Ibid.
31. Ibid.
32. Kornwolf, *Architecture and Town Planning.*
33. Jackson, *Century of Dishonor.*
34. Ibid.
35. Ibid.
36. Kennedy, *American Indian Places.*
37. Roosevelt, *Complete Works of Theodore Roosevelt.*
38. Kornwolf, *Architecture and Town Planning.*

Chapter 3

39. Jordan, "People of Ohio's First County."
40. Ibid.
41. Ibid.

42. More than they could actually afford, but the Scioto Company and others purchased the rest.
43. Summers, *History of Marietta.*
44. Andrews, *History of Marietta Washington County.*
45. Summers, *History of Marietta.*
46. Ibid.
47. National Archives, "From George Washington to Richard Henderson."
48. Andrews, *History of Marietta Washington County.*
49. Summers, *History of Marietta.*
50. Ibid.
51. Andrews, *History of Marietta Washington County.*
52. Jordan, "People of Ohio's First County."
53. Ibid.
54. Summers, *History of Marietta.*
55. Dickinson, *Century of Church Life.*

Chapter 4

56. Howe, *Historical Collections of Ohio.*
57. Parsons, "Historic Worthington."
58. Ibid.
59. Ibid.
60. Lisska, *Granville, Ohio.*
61. Parsons, "Historic Worthington."
62. Meyers and Meyers Walker, *Historic Columbus Crimes.*
63. Worthington Historical Society, "National Register of Historic Places: Thirty-one Worthington Sites."
64. Ibid.
65. Howe, *Historical Collections of Ohio.*

Chapter 5

66. Burke and Bensch, *Mount Pleasant and the Early Quakers of Ohio.*
67. Ibid.
68. Lindley, "Quaker Settlement of Ohio."
69. Burke and Bensch, *Mount Pleasant and the Early Quakers of Ohio.*

70. The original Short Creek Hicksite meetinghouse still stands in nearby Emerson.
71. Lindley, "Quaker Settlement of Ohio."
72. Ibid.
73. Burke and Bensch, *Mount Pleasant and the Early Quakers of Ohio*.
74. Thomas, "Jesse Thomas."
75. Burke and Bensch, *Mount Pleasant and the Early Quakers of Ohio*.
76. Lindley, "Quaker Settlement of Ohio."
77. Ibid.
78. Burke and Bensch, *Mount Pleasant and the Early Quakers of Ohio*.
79. Zang, *Fleet Walker's Divided Heart*.

Chapter 6

80. Lisska, *Granville, Ohio*.
81. Granville Historical Society, "Granville, Ohio Is a Special Place."
82. Granville Township was laid out in a five-mile square, rather than the customary six-mile square, owing to an act of Congress in 1796.
83. Lisska, *Granville, Ohio*.
84. Utter, *Granville*.
85. Ibid.
86. Lisska, *Granville, Ohio*.
87. Meyers and Meyers Walker, *Lynching and Mob Violence in Ohio*.
88. Lisska, *Granville, Ohio*.
89. Granville Bicentennial Committee, "Historic Homes of Granville, Ohio."
90. Ibid.

Chapter 7

91. Evans and Stivers, *History of Adams County*.
92. Ibid.
93. Birney, *James G. Birney and His Times*.
94. Meyers and Meyers Walker, *Historic Black Settlements of Ohio*.
95. Ibid.
96. Prior to the construction of dams to help control flooding, the Ohio River was from three to fifteen feet deep.
97. *History of Brown County*.

98. Parker, *His Promised Land.*
99. Ibid.
100. Hagedorn, *Beyond the River.*
101. *History of Brown County.*
102. Calarco, *Places of the Underground Railroad.*
103. Ibid.
104. Ibid.
105. Calarco, *Places of the Underground Railroad.*
106. Parker, *His Promised Land.*
107. Parker, *His Promised Land.*

Chapter 8

108. Meyers et al., *Columbus, the Musical Crossroads.*
109. Lee, *History of the City of Columbus.*
110. Lentz, *Columbus, the Story of a City.*
111. Ohio History Connection, "Columbus, Ohio."
112. By comparison, Williamsburg, Virginia, is 301 acres, but it was financed by John D. Rockefeller Jr.
113. German Village, "History."
114. Lee, *History of the City of Columbus.*
115. Ibid.
116. Ibid.
117. Williams, *German Village Guidelines.*
118. City of Columbus, "German Village Commission."
119. German Village, "History."
120. Although they take place in California, her earliest Kinsey Millhone novels were written in Columbus.

Chapter 9

121. Bahmer, *Centennial History of Coshocton County.*
122. Misencik, *American Indians of the Ohio Country.*
123. Hill, *History of Coshocton County.*
124. Ibid.
125. Ibid.
126. Bahmer, *Centennial History of Coshocton County.*

127. Hill, *History of Coshocton County*.
128. Ibid.
129. Ibid.
130. Bahmer, *Centennial History of Coshocton County*.
131. Hill, *History of Coshocton County*.
132. Ibid.
133. Roscoe Village, "History."
134. Williams, "Commitment Drives Roscoe's Rebirth."

Chapter 10

135. Meyers, *Glance of Heaven*.
136. Ibid.
137. Dobbs, *Freedom's Will*.
138. Many Christian sects such as the Mormons and the Millerites (Seventh-day Adventists) believed this.
139. Meyers, *Glance of Heaven*.
140. Nordhoff, *Communistic Societies of the United States*.
141. Meyers, *Glance of Heaven*.
142. Morhart, *Zoar Story*.
143. Meyers, *Glance of Heaven*.
144. Hinds, *American Communities*.
145. Meyers, *Glance of Heaven*.
146. Knortz, *From the Portfolio of a German-American*.

Chapter 11

147. Encyclopedia of Cleveland History, "Western Reserve."
148. Ibid.
149. Wikipedia, "Joseph Smith."
150. Smith, *Doctrine and Covenants*, 38:32–33.
151. The Mormons also settled another community in Ohio, Thompson.
152. Staker, *Hearken, O Ye People*.
153. *Urbana (OH) Citizen and Gazette*, "Mormon Emigrants."
154. Staker, *Hearken, O Ye People*.
155. Ibid.
156. Ibid.
157. Ibid.

Chapter 12

158. Kornblith, *Elusive Utopia.*
159. Ibid.
160. Ibid.
161. Ibid.
162. Ibid.
163. Ibid.
164. Two trustees elected to resign.
165. Kornblith, *Elusive Utopia.*
166. Lasser, "Oberlin College."
167. Meyers and Meyers Walker, *Reverse Underground Railroad in Ohio.*
168. Kornblith, *Elusive Utopia.*
169. Ibid.
170. Kornblith, *Elusive Utopia.*
171. Lasser, "Oberlin College."
172. Kornblith, *Elusive Utopia.*

Chapter 13

173. Lee, *History of the City of Columbus.*
174. Ibid.
175. W.B. Brooks, another wealthy coal baron, did likewise.
176. *Highland Weekly News*, March 14, 1872.
177. Reeves, "Haydenville."
178. Ibid.
179. Ibid.
180. *Hocking Sentinel*, "Death of Peter Hayden."
181. Reeves, "Haydenville."
182. Ibid.

Chapter 14

183. Built on the site of the original Ohio Penitentiary, it still stands and is worth a visit.
184. Bush, "Taps for Fort Hayes."
185. Wikipedia, "Fort Hayes."

186. Meyers and Meyers Walker, *Columbus State Community College*.
187. McChristian, *Regular Army O!*
188. Wikipedia, "Fort Hayes."
189. *City of Columbus, the Capital of Ohio*.
190. McChristian, *Regular Army O!*
191. Ibid.
192. *Columbus, the Capital City*.
193. *Columbus Dispatch*, "Average of 125 Men Handled Daily."
194. Karsko, "Crisis Adds New Page."
195. Wikipedia, "Fort Hayes."
196. Bush, "Taps for Fort Hayes."
197. Karsko, "Crisis Adds New Page."
198. Ibid.
199. Hoover, "Army Unit Honored at New Center."

Chapter 15

200. Richardson, *Brief History of Tuscarawas County*.
201. Manfield, *History of Tuscarawas County*.
202. Ibid.
203. Richardson, *Brief History of Tuscarawas County*.
204. Ibid.
205. Ibid.
206. Manfield, *History of Tuscarawas County*.
207. Meyers and Meyers Walker, *Ohio's Black Hand Syndicate*.
208. Ferguson, "War Relic."
209. Ibid.
210. *Wilmington (OH) News-Journal*, "Water Stop for Train Is Dreamville for Soldiers."
211. North Platte, Nebraska, and New York City's State Door Canteen were both larger, but neither was preserved.
212. Dennison Railroad Depot Museum, "National Historic Landmark."
213. *Sunday Times Signal*, "Zanesville Salvation Army Captain Won Fame."
214. Ibid.
215. Dennison Railroad Depot Museum, "National Historic Landmark."

Chapter 16

216. This was near the site of present-day Central Park.
217. Lakeside Chautauqua, "About Lakeside, Ohio."
218. Gasley, *Grand Assembly*.
219. Miller's fortune came from his invention of an improved combine. His daughter, Mina, would marry another Ohio inventor, Thomas Alva Edison.
220. Vincent's interest in self-education arose out of the fact that he never attended college.
221. Gasley, *Grand Assembly*.
222. Ibid.
223. Ibid.
224. Ibid.
225. Ibid.
226. Chautauqua Trail, "Chautauqua Community."
227. Gasley, *Grand Assembly*.
228. "Lakeside Chautauqua, "About Lakeside, Ohio."
229. Ibid.
230. Winter, *History of Northwest Ohio*.
231. Ketter, "Lakeside."
232. Ibid.
233. Ibid.
234. Durr, *Lakeside Lore*.
235. Determeyer, *Rhythm Is Our Business*.
236. Trusty, "Lakeside Brews Up Year Around Interest."
237. Durr, *Lakeside Lore*.
238. Lakeside Chautauqua, "About Lakeside, Ohio."

Chapter 17

239. Gase, "Man Named Ohio."
240. City of Barberton, Ohio, "History."
241. Ibid.
242. Ibid.
243. United States Department of the Interior, "Tuscarawas Avenue."
244. City of Barberton, Ohio, "History."
245. Gase, "Man Named Ohio."

Chapter 18

246. Doyle, *Centennial History of Summit County.*
247. Ibid.
248. *Akron (OH) Beacon Journal*, "Mrs. Cooley Gives $25,000 to Hiram."
249. Miller, "Jaite Mill Historic District."
250. Doyle, *Centennial History of Summit County.*
251. Ibid.
252. *Paper Trade Journal*, "Hold Up Men Get Paper Mill Pay Roll."
253. Cuyahoga Valley National Park, "Jaite, a Paper Mill and Company Town."
254. Ibid.
255. *Pittsburgh (PA) Daily Post*, "Torn to Pieces in Shafting."
256. *Paper Industry*, "Observations of a Traveler."
257. *Akron (OH) Beacon Journal*, "Peninsula."
258. There are period buildings still standing in Boston and Peninsula.
259. Cuyahoga Valley National Park, "Jaite, a Paper Mill and Company Town."
260. Ibid.
261. Cleveland Voices, "Tom and Bertha Jones Interview."
262. Ibid., "Josephine Davis Interview."
263. Cuyahoga Valley National Park, "Jaite, a Paper Mill and Company Town."
264. Doyle, *Centennial History of Summit County.*
265. On June 7, 1938, Robert's neighbor, Frank Sledz, shot and killed his wife and then himself at his home—a twenty-two-room mansion—which he operated as a roadside lunchroom. Robert said that he had never heard them quarrel.
266. *Wilmington (CA) Daily Press Journal*, "Jaite Paper Bag Company."
267. Cuyahoga Valley National Park, "Jaite, a Paper Mill and Company Town."

Chapter 19

268. Condon, *Cleveland.*
269. Ibid.
270. Ibid.
271. Ibid.

272. Ibid.
273. Chandra, "True Story of the Integration of Shaker Heights."
274. Ibid.
275. Ibid.
276. Ibid.
277. Ibid.
278. Wikipedia, "Shaker Heights, Ohio."
279. Maago, "Suburb Looks Nervously."

Chapter 20

280. Rybczynski, *City Life.*
281. Ibid.
282. Drozda, "Stroll through the Planned Community of Mariemont."
283. Ibid.
284. Rybczynski, *City Life.*
285. Parks, *Mariemont Story.*
286. Rogers, *John Nolen and Mariemont.*
287. Parks, *Mariemont Story.*
288. Rogers, *John Nolen and Mariemont.*
289. Parks, *Mariemont Story.*
290. Ibid.
291. Drozda, "Stroll through the Planned Community of Mariemont."
292. Ibid.
293. Parks, *Mariemont Story.*
294. Drozda, "Stroll through the Planned Community of Mariemont."
295. Parks, *Mariemont Story.*
296. Rogers, *John Nolen and Mariemont.*
297. Ibid.
298. Ibid.

Chapter 21

299. Suess, "Greenhills Was a New Deal Town."
300. Swartsell, "Incomplete Utopia."
301. The equivalent of $251 million in 2023.
302. Suess, "Greenhills Was a New Deal Town."

303. Swartsell, "Incomplete Utopia."
304. Ibid.
305. Suess, "Greenhills Was a New Deal Town."
306. Baca, "New Deal Landmark that's Cannibalizing Itself."
307. Sullebarger, "Greenhills Historic District."
308. Swartsell, "Incomplete Utopia."
309. Ibid.
310. Gross, "Forgotten History."
311. Swartsell, "Incomplete Utopia."
312. Suess, "Greenhills Was a New Deal Town."
313. Baca, "New Deal Landmark that's Cannibalizing Itself."
314. Swartsell, "Incomplete Utopia."
315. Ibid.
316. Ibid.
317. Ibid.
318. Ibid.
319. Sullebarger, "Greenhills Historic District."
320. Baca, "New Deal Landmark that's Cannibalizing Itself."

Afterword

321. Lincoln, *Vice President in Charge of Revolution.*
322. Ibid.
323. There is a Carl Frye Park to commemorate him.

BIBLIOGRAPHY

Books

Andrews, Martin R. *History of Marietta Washington County, Ohio*. Chicago, IL: Biographical Publishing Company, 1902.

Bahmer, William J. *Centennial History of Coshocton County, Ohio*. Chicago, IL: S.J. Clarke Publishing Company, 1909.

Birney, William. *James G. Birney and His Times*. New York: D. Appleton and Company, 1890.

Burke, James, and Donald E. Bensch. *Mount Pleasant and the Early Quakers of Ohio*. Columbus: Ohio Historical Society, 1994.

Calarco, Tom. *Places of the Underground Railroad*. Santa Barbara, CA: ABC-CLIO, LLC, 2011.

The City of Columbus, the Capital of Ohio and the Great Railway Center of the State Issued by the Columbus Board of Trade. Columbus, OH: G.L. Manchester, 1885.

Columbus, the Capital City. Columbus, OH: Pen and Pencil Club, 1915.

Condon, George. *Cleveland: The Best Kept Secret*. New York: Doubleday, 1967.

Determeyer, Eddy. *Rhythm Is Our Business*. Ann Arbor: University of Michigan Press, 2006.

Dickinson, C.W. *A Century of Church Life*. Marietta, OH: E.R. Alderman & Sons, 1896.

Dobbs, Catherine R. *Freedom's Will*. New York: William-Frederick Press, 1947.

Doyle, William B. *Centennial History of Summit County, Ohio*. Chicago, IL: Biographical Publishing Company, 1908.

Durr, Eleanor. *Lakeside Lore*. Hicksville, NY: Exposition Press, 1979.

Evans, Nelson W., and Emmons B. Stivers. *A History of Adams County, Ohio*. West Union, OH: E.B. Stivers, 1900.

Gasley, Mary. *The Grand Assembly*. Sun City, CA: Winlock Publishing Company, 1981.

Gibbon, Guy. *Archaeology of Prehistoric Native American: An Encyclopedia*. New York: Routledge, 2019.

Hagedorn, Ann. *Beyond the River*. New York: Simon & Schuster, 2002.

Hatcher, Harlan. *The Western Reserve: The Story of New Connecticut in Ohio*. New York: Bobbs-Merrill Company, 1949.

Hill, N.N., Jr. *History of Coshocton County, Ohio*. Newark, OH: A.A. Graham & Company, 1881.

Hinds, William Alfred. *American Communities*. Oneida, NY: Office of the American Socialist, 1878.

The History of Brown County, Ohio. Chicago, IL: W.H. Beers & Company, 1883.

Howe, Henry. *Historical Collections of Ohio*. Columbus, OH: Henry Howe & Son, 1891.

Jackson, Helen Hunt. *A Century of Dishonor*. New York: Harper & Brothers, 1881.

Kennedy, Frances H. *American Indian Places*. Boston, MA: Houghton Mifflin Harcourt, 2008.

Knortz, Karl. *From the Portfolio of a German-American*. Bamberg, Germany, 1893. A translation of *Aus der Mappe eines DeutschfAmerikaners*.

Kornblith, Gary J., and Carol Lasser. *Elusive Utopia*. Baton Rouge: Louisiana University Press, 2018.

Kornwolf, James D. *Architecture and Town Planning in Colonial North America*. Baltimore, MD: Johns Hopkins University Press, 2002.

Lee, Alfred E. *History of the City of Columbus*. New York: Munsell & Company, 1892.

Lentz, Ed. *Columbus, the Story of a City*. Charleston, SC: Arcadia Publishing, 2003.

Lincoln, Murray D. *Vice President in Charge of Revolution*. New York: McGraw-Hill, 1960.

Lisska, Anthony, and Louis I. Middleman, eds. *Granville, Ohio: A Purpose, a Plan, a Place*. Granville, OH: Denison University Press, 2004.

Manfield, J.B., ed. *History of Tuscarawas County, Ohio*. Chicago, IL: Warner, Beers & Company, 1884.

McChristian, Douglas C. *Regular Army O!* Norman: University of Oklahoma Press, 2017.

McLeod, Alexus. *Astronomy in the Ancient World*. Storrs, CT: Springer, 2016.

McManamon, Francis P., Linda S. Cordell, Kent G. Lightfoot and George R. Milner. *Archaeology in America*. Westport, CT: Greenwood Press, 2009.

Meyers, David. *A Glance of Heaven*. Columbus, OH: Exploding Stove, 2015.

Meyers, David, and Elise Meyers Walker. *Columbus State Community College: An Informal History*. Columbus, OH: Exploding Stove, 2013.

———. *Historic Black Settlements of Ohio*. Charleston, SC: The History Press, 2020.

———. *Historic Columbus Crimes: Mama's in the Furnace, The Thing, and More*. Charleston, SC: The History Press, 2010.

———. *Lynching and Mob Violence in Ohio*. Jefferson, NC: McFarland & Company, 2019.

———. *Ohio's Black Hand Syndicate: The Birth of Organized Crime in America*. Charleston, SC: The History Press, 2021.

———. *The Reverse Underground Railroad in Ohio*. Charleston, SC: The History Press, 2022.

Meyers, David, Arnett Howard, Jim Loeffler and Candice Watkins. *Columbus, the Musical Crossroads*. Charleston, SC: Arcadia Publishing, 2008.

Misencik, Paul R., and Sally E. Misencik. *American Indians of the Ohio Country in the 18th Century*. Jefferson, NC: McFarland & Company, 2020.

Morhart, Hilda Dischinger. *The Zoar Story*. Dover, OH, 1967.

Nordhoff, Charles. *The Communistic Societies of the United States*. New York, 1966.

Parker, John P. *His Promised Land*. New York: W.W. Norton & Company, 1996.

Parks, Warren Wright. *The Mariemont Story*. Cincinnati, OH: Creative Writers & Publishers Inc., 1967.

Reitz, Elizabeth J., C. Margaret Scarry and Sylvia J. Scudder, eds. *Case Studies in Environmental Archaeology*. 2nd ed. New York: Springer, 2008.

Richardson, J.M. *A Brief History of Tuscarawas County, Ohio*. Canal Dover, OH: Bixler Printing Company, 1896.

Rogers, Millard F., Jr. *John Nolen and Mariemont*. Baltimore, MD: Johns Hopkins University Press, 2001.

Roosevelt, Theodore. *Complete Works of Theodore Roosevelt*. Hastings, UK: Delphi Classics, 2021.

Rybczynski, Witold. *City Life*. New York: Simon & Schuster, 1995.

Smith, Joseph. *The Doctrine and Covenants of the Church of Jesus Christ of the Latter-Day Saints*. Salt Lake City, UT: Church of Jesus Christ of the Latter-day Saints, 1921.

Staker, Mark Lyman. *Hearken, O Ye People*. Salt Lake City, UT: Greg Kofford Books, 2009.

Summers, Thomas J. *History of Marietta*. Marietta, OH: Leader Publishing Company, 1903.

Thomas, David Hurst. *Exploring Ancient Native America*. New York: Routledge, 1999.

Utter, William T. *Granville: The Story of an Ohio Village*. Granville, OH: Granville Historical Society, 1956.

Williams, Judith B. *German Village Guidelines*. Columbus, OH: German Village Society, 1989.

Winter, Nevin O. *History of Northwest Ohio*. Chicago, IL: Lewis Publishing Company, 1917.

Zang, David W. *Fleet Walker's Divided Heart*. Lincoln: University Nebraska Press, 1991.

Articles

Aloia, Sara Rose. "Archaeology as Restoration: A Model from SunWatch Indian Village/Archaeological Park." Master's thesis, Ohio University, 2004.

Akron (OH) Beacon Journal. "Mrs. Cooley Gives $25,000 to Hiram." February 28, 1911.

———. "Peninsula." April 21, 1917.

Baca, Alex. "The New Deal Landmark that's Cannibalizing Itself." Bloomberg: CityLab, January 31, 2018. https://www.bloomberg.com/news/articles/2018-01-31/the-utopian-vision-of-greenhills-ohio-is-crumbling.

Bush, Bill. "Taps for Fort Hayes." *Columbus (OH) Dispatch*, March 1, 2007.

Chandra, Chethan. "The True Story of the Integration of Shaker Heights." The Shakerite, August 24, 2021. https://shakerite.com/campus-and-city/the-true-story-of-the-integration-of-shaker-heights/24/2021.

Chautauqua Trail. "The Chautauqua Community." https://www.chautauquatrail.com/the-chautauqua-movement.

City of Barberton, Ohio. "History." http://cityofbarberton.com/279/History.

City of Columbus. "German Village Commission." https://www.columbus.gov/planning/gvc.

Cleveland Voices. "Josephine Davis Interview, 2011." https://clevelandvoices.org/items/show/2125.

———. "Tom and Bertha Jones Interview, 24 June, 2008." https://clevelandvoices.org/items/show/2057.

Columbus Dispatch. "Average of 125 Men Handled Daily." December 5, 1920.

Cuyahoga Valley National Park. "Jaite, a Paper Mill and Company Town." https://www.onlyinyourstate.com/ohio/cleveland/jaite-paper-mill-cle.

Dennison Railroad Depot Museum. "National Historic Landmark." https://dennisondepot.org/national-landmark.

Drozda, Maya. "A Stroll through the Planned Community of Mariemont." Cincinnati Preservation Association. https://cincinnatipreservation.org/a-stroll-through-the-planned-community-of-mariemont.

Encyclopedia of Cleveland History. "Western Reserve." Case Western Reserve University. https://case.edu/ech/articles/w/western-reserve#:~:text=The%20WESTERN%20RESERVE%20(aka%20New,miles%20westward%20to%20Sandusky%20Bay.

Ferguson, William A. "War Relic." *Chicago Tribune*, April 3, 1994.

Gase, Molly. "A Man Named Ohio." Akronlife, March 9, 2017. https://www.akronlife.com/education/a-man-named-ohio.

German Village. "History." https://germanvillage.com/about/history.

Gershon, Livia. "Yes, Americans Owned Land Before Columbus." JSTOR Daily, March 4, 2019. https://daily.jstor.org/yes-americans-owned-land-before-columbus.

Granville Bicentennial Committee. "Historic Homes of Granville, Ohio." 2005.

Granville Historical Society. "Granville, Ohio Is a Special Place with an Interesting History." https://www.granvillehistory.org/learn-granville-history#:~:text=Unlike%20many%20settlements%20in%20the,in%20their%20area%20was%20exhausted.

Gross, Terry. "A 'Forgotten History' of How the U.S. Government Segregated America." NPR, May 3, 2017. https://www.npr.org/2017/05/03/526655831/a-forgotten-history-of-how-the-u-s-government-segregated-america.

Highland Weekly News (Highland County, OH). March 14, 1872.

Hocking Sentinel. "Death of Peter Hayden." April 12, 1888.

Hoover, Felix. "Army Unit Honored at New Center." *Columbus (OH) Dispatch*, August 19, 1996.

Jordan, Wayne. "The People of Ohio's First County." *Ohio Archaeological and Historical Society* 49 (1940).

Karsko, Bernie. "Crisis Adds New Page to Fort Hayes History." *Columbus (OH) Dispatch*, October 11, 1990.

Ketter, Peter. "Lakeside." SAH Archipedia. https://sah-archipedia.org/buildings/OH-01-123-0037.

Lakeside Chautauqua. "About Lakeside, Ohio." https://lakesideohio.com/about-lakeside.

Lasser, Carol. "Oberlin College." Encyclopedia. https://www.encyclopedia.com/social-sciences-and-law/education/colleges-us/oberlin-college.

Lindley, Harlow. "The Quaker Settlement of Ohio." *Ohio Genealogical Quarterly* (1986).

Maago, Christopher. "A Suburb Looks Nervously at Its Urban Neighbor." *New York Times*, January 17, 2008.

Miller, Carol Poh. "Jaite Mill Historic District." National Register of Historic Places Inventory—Nomination Form, August 28, 1978.

National Archives: Founders Online. "From George Washington to Richard Henderson, 19 June 1788." https://founders.archives.gov/documents/Washington/04-06-02-0304.

Ohio History Connection: Ohio History Central. "Columbus, Ohio." http://ohiohistorycentral.org/w/Columbus,_Ohio#:~:text=Columbus%20was%20chosen%20as%20the,Dublin%2C%20Worthington%2C%20and%20Delaware.

The Paper Industry. "Observations of a Traveler" (May 1926). https://www.google.com/books/edition/The_Paper_Industry/4LofAQAAMAAJ?hl=en&gbpv=1&bsq=may,%20%201926.

Paper Trade Journal 83, no. 12. "Hold Up Men Get Paper Mill Pay Roll" (September 16, 1926).

Parsons, Mira Clarke. "Historic Worthington." *Ohio Archaeological and Historical Society Publications* 13 (1904).

Pittsburgh (PA) Daily Post. "Torn to Pieces in Shafting." November 3, 1910.

Reeves, Mary Ann. "Haydenville." SAH Archipedia. https://sah-archipedia.org/buildings/OH-01-073-0038.

Robinson, Emerson. "The First Christian Indian Church." *Dearborn (MI) Independent*, August 29, 1925.

Roscoe Village. "History." https://roscoevillage.com/history.

Suess, Jeff. "Greenhills Was a New Deal Town 80 Years Ago." *Cincinnati (OH) Enquirer*, April 1, 2019.

Sullebarger, Beth. "Greenhills Historic District." SAH Archipedia. https://sah-archipedia.org/buildings/OH-01-061-0074.

Sunday Times Signal (Zanesville, OH). "Zanesville Salvation Army Captain Won Fame as Originator of Popular Railroad Canteen." March 14, 1943.

Swartsell, Nick. "An Incomplete Utopia: Looking at the Legacy of Greenhills." *CityBeat*, January 8, 2019. https://www.citybeat.com/news/eighty-years-ago-the-federal-government-built-this-greater-cincinnati-community- as-a-kind-of-social-experiment-today-its-legacy-is-in-flux-12158131.

Thomas, Mark. "Jesse Thomas." Historic Mt. Pleasant, Ohio. https://mtp1803.org/blog/2020/09/29/jesse-thomas.

Trusty, Sheri. "Lakeside Brews Up Year Around Interest with Historic Café." *Fremont (OH) News Messenger*, October 19, 2020.

United States Department of the Interior. "Tuscarawas Avenue—Alexander Square Commercial Historic District." National Register of Historic Places Registration Form, June 26, 1990. https://www.akronlibrary.org/images/Divisions/SpecCol/images/90000755.pdf.

Urbana (OH) Citizen and Gazette. "Mormon Emigrants." July 31, 1838.

Walton, Jessie. "The Forgotten History of Ohio's Indigenous Peoples." Midstory, July 16, 2020. https://www.midstory.org/the-forgotten-history-of-ohios-indigenous-peoples.

Wikipedia. "Fort Hayes." https://en.wikipedia.org/wiki/Fort_Hayes.

———. "Joseph Smith." https://en.wikipedia.org/wiki/Joseph_Smith.

———. "Shaker Heights, Ohio." https://en.wikipedia.org/wiki/Shaker_Heights,_Ohio.

Williams, Joe. "Commitment Drives Roscoe's Rebirth." *Coshocton (OH) Tribune*, November 16, 2015.

Wilmington (CA) Daily Press Journal. "Jaite Paper Bag Company." December 28, 1942.

Wilmington (OH) News-Journal. "Water Stop for Train Is Dreamville for Soldiers." April 3, 1943.

Worthington Historical Society. "National Register of Historic Places: Thirty-One Worthington Sites." http://worthingtonhistory.org/national-register-of-historic-places.

Worthington Memory. "Brief History of Bill Moose." http://www.worthingtonmemory.org/scrapbook/text/brief-history-bill-moose#:~:text=Bill%20Moose%20was%20believed%20to,by%20people%20throughout% 20central%20Ohio.

Zepp, E.C. "By the Beautiful Spring." *Regional Review* 5, no. 1 (July 1940).

INDEX

A

B

C

D

E

F

G

H

I

J

K

L

M

N

O

P

Q

R

S

T

Z

ABOUT THE AUTHORS

A graduate of Miami and Ohio State Universities, DAVID MEYERS has written numerous local histories, as well as works for the stage and a handful of historical novels, including *Hello, I Must Be Going* and *Ball of Confusion*. David was inducted into the Ohio Senior Citizens Hall of Fame for his contributions to local history. ELISE MEYERS WALKER is a graduate of Hofstra and Ohio Universities. She has collaborated with her father on more than a dozen local histories, including *Lynching and Mob Violence in Ohio*, *Historic Black Settlements of Ohio*, *The Reverse Underground Railroad in Ohio* and *A Murder in Amish Ohio*. Both David and Elise are available for presentations. The authors' website is www.explodingstove.com, or readers can follow them on Twitter, YouTube, Facebook and Instagram @explodingstove.